PROFESSIONALISM
Your EDGE in the Job Market

© 2011 by Kaplan, Inc.

Published by Kaplan Publishing,

a division of Kaplan, Inc.

395 Hudson Street, 4th Floor

New York, NY 10014

Permissions

Cover photos reproduced by permission from Getty/Blend Images; Jupiter Images; Getty Images/Fuse; Getty Images/Go Go Images RF.

Printed in the United States of America

10 9 8 7 6 5 4 3

ISBN-13: 978-1-60714-958-3

Contents

Introduction

Congratulations, you've taken the first step toward your new career! By starting a new higher education program, you have made a commitment to developing the core skills that are required to grow in your chosen career. We admire your dedication to building your own success story.

You may think that you are going back to school just to learn the skills or competencies that are necessary to perform on the job. For example, a health student may learn how to perform injections properly; a trades student might learn how to install an electrical outlet safely; or a criminal justice student might learn how to fingerprint correctly. In your program, you will have the opportunity to learn the hands-on practices that are current in your chosen career. However, in your Kaplan Higher Education program, you will learn much more. The Kaplan Advantage℠ is not only about learning the hands-on skills you will need on the job, but also about practicing the critical professional behaviors that can make the difference between getting the job and being the next in line.

What do employers say about who wins the job?

Kaplan's researchers interviewed employers across the careers for which we prepare students, and asked them, "What makes the difference between the person you hire and the person you don't?" Their answers were surprisingly consistent across a wide variety of fields, including health care, trades, criminal justice, business, and the arts. In this book, in the professionalism lessons in your courses, and in your meetings with campus staff, you will have the opportunity to learn what employers told us about how to get an edge over others who are competing for the same job.

We also asked employers, "What makes the difference between the employee you value and promote and the person you eventually let go?" We will also share those very important lessons, so you can use the Kaplan Advantage to build the rest of your career, long after graduation.

So what's the bottom line?

Summarized to the simplest points, employers told us that, yes, job skills are very important—you can't get the job without them—but for every job, they see several candidates who have the required skills. So how do they decide who gets the job? Employers look for candidates who have the Four Pillars of Professionalism. Those individuals are:

E = **Empowered**

D = **Dependable**

G = **Goal-Oriented**

E = **Engaged**

We will give a brief explanation of the Four Pillars here, but you will learn a great deal more about them in this book, and you will have an opportunity to practice them in your classes and in sessions with campus staff.

Empowered. Employers are attracted to candidates who look the part and act the part. The most obvious way to look the part is to dress correctly. The rules for interview and work attire vary by field, so it is important to get advice from someone who has worked in the career for a long time. The best resource is someone who has hired and managed many people in the field. At your campus, there are several reliable resources, including your instructor and several school staff members, who will be happy to provide advice. Attire is just the simplest aspect of empowerment, however. The empowered candidate also is confident, smiles, and looks others in the eye. In this book and in your classes, you will have the opportunity to learn the strategies for becoming empowered.

Dependable. You can do a great job only if you are actually there to do the job! This may seem obvious, but employers tell us repeatedly that many employees ruin their chances at winning the job (or at advancement once they have the job) simply because they fail to show up on time (or even to show up at all). If you want to impress your boss, you need to be dependable; you need to show up every time, on time. If the employer can count on you, then you will eventually be given more responsibility and will have the chance to move forward in your career.

Goal-Oriented. Many employees think that they are doing a good job if they are following their supervisor's instructions. Our interviews with employers tell us that this is true, but only to a point. Employers do want employees to do as they are told—the first or second time—but after that, employers want employees to be able to figure out what needs to be done on their own. Employers say that the best employees do what needs to be done without being told—they have initiative. If you can put yourself in your employer's shoes and recognize the goal, you can show that you are goal-oriented by working toward that goal on your own.

Engaged. The best employees know that it's not about their individual goals—it's about the team. So, employers tell us that they like people who are engaged, who really work well with others. This is just as important for people who work in the trades, where small teams must work very closely together at distant work sites, as it is for people who work in hospitals and large companies, where large teams must collaborate at central locations. If you're not seen as a team player, you're not going to have an edge. So how can you build your EDGE and experience the Kaplan Advantage? This book will teach you everything you need to know.

You are the key to unlocking your talent!

Keep in mind that your career requires more from you than simply memorizing facts that you will learn in this book. Reading the material presented in this book is an essential step toward getting what you want in your life, but it's up to you to make it work. You have to see the big picture. Simply put, you need to understand that you are now in sales. Everyone looking for a job is a salesperson. And the product that you are selling is you! In order to sell yourself effectively, you must be aware of how other people perceive you. You have to understand how you come across in a meeting, on the street, and over the phone. You need to take responsibility for your image and actively manage it. In order to be a good salesperson, you need to figure out how to produce the results you are looking for. Here are some steps that will help you get those results.

First, commit to school and growing your talent. You have taken the first step by enrolling; now you need to be determined about removing obstacles, ignoring distractions, and getting to graduation. Take a piece of paper and write down your reason for going back to school. Put it in an important place where you will see it—on the refrigerator, on your bathroom mirror, in your notebook, in your phone case. Keep your reason as a constant reminder of why you need to overcome distractions and keep going when the going gets tough.

Second, when you walk into the classroom, it's a whole new you. Your classroom is the dress rehearsal for your job—think of your Kaplan Higher Education campus as your new employer. Don't think of any of your courses as "just a class," but look at each class as the first step toward your new career. This is your future! Don't fall back into your old school patterns. You have to conduct yourself professionally while you are a student. Professionalism is a skill that is learned through practice. If you go to school every day and practice being a clown, you're going to have a really hard time being anything but a joker when you enter the workplace. Instead, act like a professional powerhouse at school. This new attitude will help you take advantage of the talent you already have.

Third, give your all to this program and make every second of it count. You are here because you want something larger for yourself. Stay focused and put in the time. Your courses will provide you the opportunity to realize your full potential. If you put in the time, your studies can have an amazing impact on your professional career. Your Kaplan Higher Education campus is going to support you the entire way. Now is the time to put your head down and get everything you can out of it.

We are here to help

You will use this book in every course in your program. Each unit will guide you through one important step in your career search and your journey toward improving your lifelong professionalism skills.

1 **Preparing for the Job Search** A crucial step in searching for a job is to step outside your point of view and into the employer's perspective. In this unit, you will learn to see yourself from an employer's point of view. You will pretend that everyone is watching and rethink your digital footprint, your email account, your voicemail messages, your ringtones, and all the other subtle messages that you send about yourself. You will learn to conduct yourself as if your future bosses are watching—because they are.

2 **Job Search Resources** Many job searchers engage in "magical thinking" about the job search: "If I think about getting a job, it will magically appear!" While there are some people who stumble upon jobs in lucky ways, most people get their jobs as a result of good, old-fashioned hard work. This unit will show you how to arrange your resources to put together your job search campaign. The search for an entry-level job typically takes several months and a whole lot of old-fashioned hard work, so gather those resources and get going. Every day counts.

3 **Resumes** You may not have experience in working in your new field, but you already have many skills. Many of the skills that you've developed over your lifetime—in your current job, in previous jobs, in your outside activities, even in the things you do for fun— are called transferable skills. These are skills that you learned in one situation that can be applied to other situations as well. Your resume is where you will highlight these skills. A well-crafted resume will outline your strengths so that employers can see exactly why you are right for a position. This unit will give you the resume *do*s and *don't*s and will show you how to put together a resume that highlights your unique skills and the qualifications you've gained from your program.

4 **Portfolios** Your resume *tells* what you can do; your portfolio *shows* what you can do. In this unit, you will learn how to develop a portfolio that showcases the skills you've developed in your program and throughout your life and career. By providing potential employers with samples of your work, you let them see exactly how well you can put your skills into practice—and how well you could put your skills to work for them.

5 **Cover Letters and Applications** Does the cover letter matter? Isn't the application just a copy of the resume in a different format? Not at all. Savvy job searchers can move up their place in line with great cover letters and applications. In this unit, we will answer common questions about cover letters and resumes and give you ideas for how to make professional cover letters that can get you noticed in a big stack of applicants.

6 **Personal Brand** Large companies like McDonald's® and Coca-Cola® spend millions of dollars to figure out how to control how we think and feel about their products. What if you could come up with a way to control how a potential employer thought about you? You may not have considered it, but you are turning yourself into a valuable product that a future employer will buy. You are in sales.

You have a "brand" to build and protect. In this unit, you will learn how to get the "product"—that is yourself—ready for the market. You will have the biggest advantage if you start building your personal brand right now.

7 Professional Presentation In this unit, we cover preparation for the interview. Remember that the employers we surveyed said that candidates need to be empowered in order to win the job? Here, we discuss how to build your image, your professional presentation. We will discuss how to dress the part, look the part, act the part, respect others, and be interested. All of these skills will help you make a great impression on people.

8 Interviews Uh-oh, the interview. Just the thought of the interview may send your pulse racing. But like many things that seem intimidating and complicated, the key to success is something small and simple: Be prepared. Not so hard, right? This unit, and exercises in class and with campus staff, will provide you with the resources you need to sharpen your interviewing skills. You will learn the importance of arriving early to signal that you are dependable and of discussing the employer's goals to demonstrate that you are goal-oriented. By knowing exactly what you can expect from a typical job interview and by rehearsing answers to key questions, you will go into every interview fully prepared and ready for a new career.

9 Follow-up and Negotiations Many candidates get very close to winning the job, only to fumble the ball during follow-up and post-interview negotiations. Candidates can miss a simple courtesy, like failing to send a thank-you note, or they may have an inflated sense of their worth and demand too high a salary or too many perks, causing an employer to turn to another candidate at the last minute. In this unit, we will cover common errors and provide tips that will help you maximize your job offers.

10 Communication and Teamwork You won the job. Congratulations! Now, how can you turn this job into a career? Remember, our employers reported that they valued and promoted employees who understood teamwork and were truly engaged. If you want to keep your job, and to have opportunities to earn more money and get broader and more exciting assignments, then you are going to need to read this unit to learn how to communicate with others and be an engaged member of the team.

11 Managing Finances You're in the money! Having a steady paycheck is an exciting place to be, especially when you have achieved a full-time job with solid benefits. In this unit, we will discuss how to manage your finances professionally. If you have student loans, how do you fit your payments into your budget in order to repay your obligations? How can you manage credit responsibly? How do people manage their way toward a debt-free position? We will discuss these questions and ways to find resources in your community.

12 Career Development Many people think career development is something that their boss or their company does, but career development is *your* responsibility. Just as you have taken charge of developing your talent by enrolling in an education program, you will need to take charge of developing your talent again once you are in the workplace. You will need to set goals, make a plan, gather resources, and network, just as you will need to do in this *Professionalism* program. In this unit, we will discuss how to practice ongoing career development so that you will have the Kaplan Advantage throughout your career, well after graduating from your program.

13 Time Management If you want to have the EDGE over your peers, you need to practice professional time management on the job. The number one thing that employers said to us over and over again (and this is true across careers, from health care through criminal justice through trades through business through arts) is that punctuality matters. Think about it: If you're not there, how can you be doing a good job? In this unit, we will talk about time management. In some ways, it's the simplest skill, but it's clearly one that trips up many employees in realizing their talent.

Your future is now

As you make your way through *Professionalism*, you will find answers to the following and many other important career-related questions. Read them now so you can look out for solutions in the book, during classroom activities, and from your instructors. Remember, your professional future starts here.

☐ How can writing down your goals help you achieve more?

☐ Why is it important to develop an effective time management plan?

☐ How can you present a positive image as you prepare for your new career?

☐ In addition to the words you choose, what other elements of communication influence meaning in a conversation?

☐ How can you improve your business writing without learning a million grammar rules?

☐ How can you engage an audience when you give a presentation?

☐ What can you do to get along with difficult co-workers and customers?

☐ How can you create a professional resume if you don't have a lot of work experience?

☐ How can you demonstrate your skills during an interview?

☐ How can strategies designed to sell products be used to help you find a job?

☐ Why is it important to have a personal statement summing up who you are and what you want?

☐ How can you develop a network of connections in your field while you are still a student?

☐ What questions are illegal to ask during an interview?

☐ What should you know about the company you're considering—beyond what it sells?

☐ How can you keep your personal biases out of the workplace?

☐ What qualities make someone a good team player?

☐ Why are ethics important in the workplace?

☐ How can employee benefits increase your bank account?

☐ What should you take away from an employee appraisal at work?

—Mel Robbins

Acknowledgments

hank you to the following editors for their contributions.

Kaplan Higher Education Corporation Chicago, Illinois

Karen Baldeschwieler, MBA, PhD
VP, Academic Programs

Sarah Croft
Manager, Research and Curriculum Design

Jon Eads, PhD
Executive Director, Research and
Curriculum Design

Chakana Fowler
Director, Curriculum Operations

Yvonne Gasik
VP, Product Development

Murray Matens Kimball
Instructional Designer

Maegan K. Murphy
Executive Director, Student Experience

Individual Kaplan Campuses

Michelle Cox and Charlotte D. Lofton, MBA
Director of Career Services
Chair, Medical Program Management Dept.
Kaplan College
Dallas/Ft. Worth
Kaplan Career Institute
Dallas, Texas
Brooklyn, Ohio

Monica Hill-Sumlin and Nova S. Pena
Director of Career Services
Kaplan College Dayton
Dayton, Ohio
Career Centers of Texas, El Paso
El Paso, Texas

Anna Howell and Greg Witkowski
Director of Career Services
Instructor Florida Education Center
Kaplan Career Institute, ICM Campus
Lauderhill, Florida
Pittsburgh, Pennsylvania

Jennifer M. Kelly, MSHR, PHR
Director
Kaplan Career Institute, ICM Campus
Pittsburgh, Pennsylvania

PROFESSIONALISM

Presenting your information in a way that supports your career goals

Obtaining the documents you need for your job search

Knowing how to put together a list of references

Ensuring that your job search documents are accurate, neatly
presented, and error-free

Knowing what to expect from background checks and drug tests

i n the movies, a job search always begins dramatically: the job seeker
opens up the classified ads and circles prospects with a thick red pen,
or begins calling companies and asking to talk to the boss.

In real life, job searches rarely work like this. Your job search actually
begins long before you read your first job ad or send out your first resume. In
fact, the more prepared you are when you start your job search, the shorter
your search is likely to be. Doing research before you start sending out
resumes will also make it more likely that the job you ultimately get is one
that suits your particular skills, personality, and goals.

This unit isn't about the job search process, but it can help you find work
in your chosen career. This unit is about what happens *before* you start the
actual job search. It's about the all-important preparation work you need to
do so your search will go smoothly. If you prepare well, you will help prospective employers to see that you are a candidate who has the EDGE that they
are seeking: Empowered, Dependable, Goal-Oriented, Engaged.

Pretend Everyone Is Watching

Before the Internet became popular, it was fairly easy for employees to keep their private lives private. However, in the digital world, everything has changed. What you post about yourself online (and whatever else someone can discover about you online) is referred to as your **digital footprint.** As technology advances and you do more and more online with Facebook, Twitter, blogs, and so forth, your digital footprint will get bigger and bigger. Since potential employers may look at the material you post online, it's important that you think carefully about the messages you are sending about yourself. Your profile on social networking sites should be PG-rated. The photos of scantily dressed people drunk at a party may be fun for friends, but if a future employer ever sees them, guess who's NOT getting the job? You! If you are seen as a wild partier, you will probably not be perceived as Dependable.

Think twice about posting strong political or religious views. It's fine to have strong views, but keep them private if there could be any chance of alienating a future employer. Conduct yourself online as if your future bosses are watching. They are. You may have had a colorful past, but if you want a professional future, don't post the evidence of it online.

If you absolutely must share your strong views and photos with your friends, then become very educated about privacy controls, and set them so that only people with permission can see your information. To make sure that you haven't made an error in your privacy settings, test them regularly from someone else's computer, and remember: the person searching for information about you is probably better at searching for information online than you are. It can be difficult to erase information

from the Internet, and it only takes a few minutes to damage your reputation. Think about the celebrities who have ruined their reputations because of a few photos that were put out on the Internet. You may not be famous, but your digital footprint matters, too.

Here are some important steps to take:

Google yourself. You can assume that one of the first things your future boss will do in determining whether to consider you for your dream job is "Google" you. So, go ahead. Google yourself and see what you find. If there is anything unattractive there, you need to be prepared to explain or counteract it. If you have a Twitter® account, your employer will likely be following you. So, watch what you say. The easiest way to do the right thing online is to pretend everyone in the world can see everything you are doing (because they probably can). If you wouldn't want your mother, your spiritual advisor, your spouse, or your employer to see what you are about to write or post, then don't do it. Take down the photos, clean up your language, and untag yourself from any compromising photos that other people have posted of you. Professionals control their public image carefully.

Get a new email account. While you may communicate with your friends using Facebook® or texting, employers still communicate by email. For professional reasons, your email address needs to be your name. So, for job search purposes, forget about the shopaholic$@gmail.com or monstertruckfan@yahoo.com or momof3kids@yahoo.com address, and create a new account with just your name. If your name is taken, add digits to the end to make it unique. Or you can use your school email address as your professional account.

Clean up your voicemail messages and ringtones. It's great that you have a favorite song, or that your little three-year-old cousin has learned to talk, but a potential employer may not want to know that, especially if the ringtone is explicit. You cannot rely on your future employer's sharing your sense of humor. Be sure that your outgoing voicemail message is very professional and that a standard ringtone is set for business calls.

> ## **True**Story
>
> "My ex-husband was mad at me for getting a restraining order against him, so he got back at me during a job interview. I had one of those phones that was also a walkie-talkie, and in the middle of my big interview, the phone barked out a curse word! It happened three times. I didn't get the job. I changed phones that same day."

Your Background

Looking for a job is always challenging, and this is especially true for new graduates and people who are changing careers. That's why it's vitally important to be as organized and prepared as possible. This means assembling the documents that prospective employers will most likely request, including:

Legal documents. You will need proof of your right to work in the United States. This means that you should locate your legal documents. It is useful to have your birth certificate or passport and your social security card. If you are a permanent resident, you will need your green card or proof of residency. If you are a veteran, you may find your discharge paperwork useful. If you have misplaced any of your legal documents, it can take some time to replace them, so get started now in putting together the documents that you need.

Transcripts. **Transcripts** list your coursework and grades for your entire time at school. A prospective employer may or may not request transcripts, but you should have an up-to-date copy of your transcripts easily available in case they are needed, especially considering that it often takes weeks to obtain them. Order your transcripts now. You can order them from your school, and most schools have an easy website form. If your school does not, simply call the registrar and ask how to obtain an official transcript. It may cost a few dollars for processing. If you have attended several schools and colleges, request a transcript from each one, unless you have transferred all of your credits from one school to another. Look at your transcripts as if you were an employer. If there is anything unusual about them, be prepared to explain it.

References. **References** are people who can vouch for your work ethic, character, or other personal qualities that make you a good job prospect. The best work reference is usually a supervisor from a previous job. If you do not have a good supervisor reference, then an instructor who has worked in the field is the next best choice. After that, a respected community member, such as a leader of a charity or service group where you have donated time, or a spiritual advisor would be a good choice. Family members and friends are not appropriate references.

Resume. Your resume is crucial. This document lists your relevant work and educational experience. Early in your career, your resume should be restricted to one page, free of grammatical errors and typos, and presented in a pleasing format, using a traditional typeface. We will work through resumes in detail in Unit 3, Resumes.

ON THE JOB

SCENARIO: You'll be graduating soon, and you are already planning the job search process. You can't think of anyone to use as a reference from your current job, because it's not in the same industry that you will be targeting in your search. What should you do?

QUICK FIX: Even if you are planning on finding work in a different field, you can still use current and former supervisors as references. They can confirm your general professionalism and dependability. You can also use people outside of work as references. Think about other people in positions of authority who might make good references, such as instructors, volunteer coordinators, coaches, and religious leaders.

Certifications, awards, and honors. Do you have any certifications, or have you won awards or honors in your field? It may take you a little time to think about these, but even certifications in first aid and CPR can be important. If you can't find a certificate, go back to the provider and ask for a replacement. Now is the time to gather your documents.

Samples of your best work. Even if nothing comes to mind right away, think about this. Ask your instructors, friends, and family if they can think of anything that represents your best work, since sometimes others are the best judges of what we do that is impressive. If you are an artist, this may be artwork. If you are in the trades, this could be an example of your best weld. Think creatively!

Check and Double-Check

Obtaining all of the necessary information and assembling these documents will take some time, so it's best to begin long before you plan on sending out your first resume—at least two months in advance. Keep all the information organized and easily accessible.

When you put together your references, try to think of four or five credible individuals to list. Employers typically ask for three references, but it's a good idea to have a few more lined up in case someone asks for more. Contact all references and get their permission before you list them; you need to check ahead of time to make sure they'll give you a good reference and to prepare them for a call from a prospective employer. Most people welcome the opportunity to serve as a reference, and it's very rare for individuals to agree to serve as your reference if they plan on giving a bad report. When you put together your list of references, make sure you include each person's name and job title, the name and address of the company where the person works, a phone number, and an email address.

Make sure that all the information in your documentation is absolutely accurate. Never "fudge" your GPA on your resume; if your prospective employer requests your transcripts from your school, your deception will be immediately exposed. Never fake a reference by asking a friend to cover for you; it's easy for a prospective employer to uncover the truth here as well.

> **True**Story
>
> "I was hiring a college instructor, and a candidate told me she had a master's degree from a local college. I called them up, and they said she had worked there for a few months but didn't even have a bachelor's degree. We were hiring her to teach; did she really think we wouldn't check?"

Drug Testing

Drug testing is a common component of job hunting and employment. Many employers routinely require drug testing for new job candidates. Industries that regularly give drug tests include construction and any other occupation that requires operation of heavy equipment; health care and allied health care professions, such as medical and dental assistant positions; and jobs in education where you'll be working closely with children. The best way to avoid losing your dream job because of a drug test is to avoid using illicit substances in the first place.

Employers use a number of technologies to perform drug tests:

- Urine analysis
- Hair analysis
- Breath analysis
- Oral fluid analysis

Of these, urine and hair tests are by far the most common. In many cases, samples for these tests are collected on-site, or in a dedicated laboratory, by a certified drug testing technician (DTT), who has experience in collecting samples and administering drug tests. These samples are typically sent to a lab that has experience in analyzing samples. In recent years, labs have grown more sophisticated, returning more positive results for people who attempted to cheat the drug test by one means or another.

Drug testing falls under state jurisdiction, which means there are no federal laws covering drug testing policy. However, most states allow employers to conduct drug testing on employees and prospective employees as part of a "drug-free workplace" policy. According to the Department of Labor, companies typically have "considerable latitude" over their drug testing policies. Most companies will keep a written "drug-free workplace" document that clearly details the company's notification policy and drug testing protocols.

Background Checks

In addition to drug testing, many employers conduct routine background checks. The Internet has made it easier than ever to dig deep into an applicant's background, so if you're worried about anything in your past, it's best to be upfront about it. During the interview process, you might be asked to give written permission for a background check; your permission gives the employer legal standing to search records covering a variety of areas:

- Employment verification
- Credit report
- Driving record
- Civil claims

- Social Security verification
- Criminal history
- Military records
- Prison record
- Workman's compensation claims
- Registered sex offender status

You have the legal right to refuse to give permission for a background check, but during the job search process this may mean you won't get the job. If you are worried about a background check, address the things that can be fixed, such as poor credit or outstanding parking tickets, and investigate whether you can erase other negative marks on your record.

KAPLAN **success** STORY

Bryan Dobao
McAllen, Texas

Attended: Kaplan College—McAllen
Area of study: Electrical Technician graduate

I knew that I had several counts of legal issues in my background; it seemed like the odds of finding employment were against me. I sat with the Director of Career Services to fill out the paperwork for my license and I discussed these issues. The Director of Career Services took the time to talk through my issues without judging and understood that I was truly a victim of circumstance. I wasn't going to let these issues set me back and neither was my Director of Career Services. With his positive attitude and the help of my instructors, I was able to get my license and get placed with an electrical company one day after graduating from Kaplan College! It is amazing what the right attitude can do!

Unit Summary

- All the materials you use in your job search, including your digital footprint, should be presented in a professional way.

- It's important to assemble all the information employers might need, including legal documents, transcripts, references, and resume, *before* you start your job search.

- A reference list should include four or five people who can speak about your professional qualifications. References generally come from instructors or past employers; friends and family members shouldn't be used as references.

- Pre-employment drug testing and background checks are routinely required by companies.

TO-DO List

✔ Clean up your **digital footprint** as much as you can, and be ready to explain anything you can't change.

✔ List five people you can use as **references,** and contact them for permission to do so.

✔ Obtain copies of your **transcripts.**

✔ Clean up your record as much as you can to remove references to credit problems and outstanding legal issues.

Important Terms

How well do you know these terms? Look them up in the glossary if you need help remembering them.

reference

transcript

digital footprint

Online Resources

Job-Search Function and Other Job-Hunting Resources
career-advice.monster.com/job-search/careers.aspx

Job Search Tips (from About.com)
jobsearch.about.com/cs/jobsearchhelp/a/jobtips.htm

Job-Hunting & Business Etiquette Resources
www.quintcareers.com/job-hunting_etiquette.html

Exercises

Write your answers on a separate piece of paper.

1. Identify a few companies where you'd like to work and write up a short profile of each, including its biggest products or services, its competitors, and who manages it. Store this information with all your job search material so that you can refer to it later.

2. Write about five things you can do to improve your list of references or your non-work background. If necessary, do some research on local opportunities for volunteering.

3. Write a one-page essay about how your job field has changed in the past ten years and how you expect it to change in the next ten years. In what ways do you expect the skills needed to enter the field to change?

Job Search Resources

KEYS TO success

Visualizing your successful future

Approaching the job search with a sales mindset

Identifying companies where you'd like to work

Keeping detailed notes on companies you are researching

Expanding your career network

Preparing a one-minute "elevator pitch" to use as a quick introduction

Being persistent and staying positive

t o be successful at anything, you need to set goals. Your career is like a road trip. To plan a road trip, you need to know two things—where you are going and how long you have to get there. The same is true with your career. Where do you want to end up, and by when? Knowing the answers to these questions will help get you closer to having a career. Let's set your goals now. These statements will help you set your goals:

My future career is _____ .

This program will help me achieve it because _____ .

My greatest strength is _____ .

I want to improve in the following ways: _____ .

Employers favor employees who are goal-oriented. These high-level goals will get you started. You will do more detailed goal setting, including setting SMART goals and creating a Career Roadmap, in your Kaplan Higher Education program. In this unit, we will focus on gathering the resources for your job search so you can achieve your immediate goal.

You Can Do This

You are the only person who can make your job search a success. The instructors and staff at your Kaplan Higher Education campus have a tremendous amount of experience and are there to help you and provide you with tools. However, if you are to be successful in your job search, you must take charge of your own future and take responsibility for developing your own talent. The job search is a big challenge, but you are up to it. Millions of people have exactly the job they want and are moving forward in their careers in ways that satisfy them. Why not you? You can meet your education and career goals and write your own success story. As you get into the job search, your approach really matters.

Here are some important tips:

Design Your Schedule for Success

School is not just going to fit into your existing schedule. To prepare for a rewarding career, you have to make the time. Planning your success starts with your calendar. Sit down now, and plan out a few blocks of time every week that you can dedicate to your future. You will use the time to study, develop a professional network, and complete tasks that will get you closer to your goal. If you live with someone, or if you have a spouse or kids, it is very important to discuss your schedule with them as well. Ask for their support. Thinking you can do this alone or in spite of them isn't going to work. They can help you stick to the schedule you are creating for yourself. Your schedule for success is a powerful tool. Design it and make yourself accountable to it. It works!

Create a Weekly Routine

The more your week falls into a routine, the easier it will be to stick to your schedule and be successful. You go to class on certain days. You study on certain days. You have family time on certain days. Keep your busy life simple by keeping your routine consistent. This is the key to success. Make time to pursue your dream by making that time easier to find. Make your routine a priority. We will talk in more detail about time management strategies in Unit 13.

Visualize Your Future

This sounds cheesy, and maybe it is. The funny thing is, it works. Think about it: Before you go to the grocery store, you make a list of the ingredients for specific meals you envision creating in the days ahead. You then go get those items. That saves time (and money). You are planning a small part of your future. You are crystal clear about what you want. When you "see" or plan for something, you actually have something to strive for. The same works for your Future You. Plan for the future, and start planning by visualizing the Future You.

Find a picture in a magazine that represents your future. It could be a picture of someone in your newly chosen field, or a photo you take of the building you hope to work in, or something you plan to buy yourself as a reward when you finish the course and land a job. This is your shopping list for your career. This is what you want. This is what you are working toward. As corny as you feel, find the picture and stick it on the wall where you study. Whenever you want to, look up and let the picture remind you of what you are working toward. Ask yourself the following questions: Where do you picture yourself in the next one, two, five, ten years? How will a new career help you reach those goals? You are visualizing the future you are actively creating for yourself. Nice.

Take on a Sales Mindset

You are the salesperson, and the product you are selling is yourself. So, how do you get started? Great salespeople know that they are going to have to lose a lot of potential sales in order to win a few. You have probably heard that salespeople have thick skins or are very persistent. That's because they have to get used to hearing the word "no." In fact, salespeople usually hear "no" 20 to 30 times as often as they hear "yes"!

As an example, let's follow an imaginary car salesperson. The picture below shows the "sales funnel," which is the process that a salesperson follows. Our imaginary salesperson needs to sell 20 cars per month.

Car Sales Model

Leads	**1,000**
Contacts	**800**
Visits	**400**
Test Drives	**300**
Offers	**100**
Sales	**20**

A **lead** is a person who is interested in buying something. For example, if a customer goes to the car dealer's website and fills out a form with name, address, and phone number, then that customer becomes a lead. Believe it or not, in this example, our salesperson needs to have 1,000 leads in order to sell the required 20 cars. Let's see how this works. The car dealer puts out some advertisements and gets

1,000 people to send in forms (1,000 leads). The salesperson goes to the phone and calls all the phone numbers (That's about 40 calls a day!). If the salesperson reaches about 8 of 10 leads, then that's 800 contacts. Let's say the salesperson is very convincing and gets about half of the people contacted to come in and look at a car, so that's 400 visits. We already know the salesperson is terrific, so of the 400 people who come in, 300 of them decide to take a test drive, so that's 300 test drives. Because those cars are really great, 1 in 3 test drivers decides to make an offer, so that's 100 offers. Let's say the finances work out and the offer is right for about 1 in 5 of the offers, so our salesperson makes a deal 20 percent of the time, for a total of 20 deals. Phew! Look at all the hard work that goes into the salesperson's making quota.

There's no luck or magic about it—it's just math. Great salespeople know that if they work hard enough and they can stand to hear the word "no", they will meet their goal.

You can, too! Job searching is nothing more than personal sales. There is no luck or magic to it. People who prepare properly, do their research, and work hard can do the math, just like salespeople. Fortunately, you need to make only one sale, not 20 per month. You need only one job! So, the numbers for your job search are smaller than the salesperson's numbers:

Personal Sales Model

Job Leads	**300**
Calls	**30**
Callbacks	**20**
Interviews	**10**
Offers	**2**
Jobs	**1**

You are going to need something like 300 good leads on desirable jobs in order to win your job. The exact number varies depending on how rare the job is that you desire, how difficult the employment market is when you are searching, and many other factors. However, the overall principles do not change: You need a *lot* of job leads before you will complete your job search, and you will (most likely) have to deal with some disappointment. Just think like a

salesperson—each rejection gets you one step closer to your big win! Here's how it works. If you get 300 good leads on desirable jobs, then you can send in 300 great cover letters and resumes. The odds are only 10 percent at best that an employer will call you on a cold cover letter and resume sent in response to an online posting. So, for 300 cover letters and resumes, you should expect about 30 calls. If you get called, chances are about 1 in 3 that you can get to an interview, so that's about 10 interviews. It takes about 5 interviews to get a good offer. So, you really have to expect at least 4 rejections before you'll find your job. If you do better than that, you are beating the odds.

Are you scared? That's not surprising. Searching for a job is one of the greatest challenges that each of us faces in life. However, if you think like a salesperson, you should feel better—it's really just math. If you are realistic about your options, and if you put in enough time and effort, you will secure a good job. The most important thing to remember as you start your job search is to keep an even keel and not get frustrated. The salesperson knows that every "no" brings you one step closer to the "yes." Take on a sales mindset: You are selling yourself, and you are a great product!

TrueStory

"I graduated in 1988, and it was one of the worst job markets in a long time. I remember I sent out more than 350 resumes and cover letters. In the months before graduation, we were all really scared, so we tried to make it fun. We wallpapered our rooms with rejection letters and made it a contest to see who could get the most! We all got jobs, but it was really hard."

Researching Job Leads

Before you begin researching, it is important to get an overview of your industry so that you know where to look. It is critical to develop relationships with people who work in the field to learn more about how it works.

Learn About Your Field

You will need a mentor to tell you more about your chosen career. As you begin your research into places to work, you are likely to have many questions. The instructors and staff at your Kaplan Higher Education campus are terrific resources to help you understand the way your industry works, who the employers are in your area, and which employers might be a good fit for your interests. Don't be shy. Your instructors teach because they want to help you succeed and because they want to help you grow your talent. They also have worked in the field and have information that will help you in your new career. They may be willing to serve as references or help you network. You should definitely get to know them. How do you do that? Simple: show up for class and be interested. Ask questions after class. Email questions during the week. Ask your instructor for advice about finding a mentor. The more enthusiasm you show for the coursework and your future, the faster you'll create that relationship. Believe it or not, this is a very important skill. Great professionals learn how to create relationships.

Here's an important tip: If you are interested in people, they will find you interesting. Being interested in them means asking them questions, giving them your full attention, and maintaining eye contact with them.

Here are some other simple techniques you should master to help you become more effective at building relationships:

Listen. Connecting with people is all about listening, not talking. When you are listening, you are learning what the other person needs, wants, and is interested in. You can and should use this information to help you forge a relationship with the person, which can help you get what you want.

Ask a question. Remember some small detail about the person or something from the conversation. Next time you see him or her, bring it up. *Is your daughter feeling better? How'd that interview go? Hey, I remembered the name of that book we were talking about. Did you land the business?* Show that you remember anything at all, no matter how small. By doing so, you will make the other

person feel important (because you remembered something), and you will create continuity from the first conversation. This makes your connection that much more meaningful.

Find a mentor. A mentor is someone who will help you grow in any area of your career. Anyone can be your mentor, not just an instructor. So, keep an open mind as to who this person might be. Look for someone who has the skills, experience, or traits that you want to cultivate in yourself. Look for someone who is doing the job you would love or who works in the industry you hope to break into. Ask people if they know anyone who does what you want to do. You want to talk to that person. People like to talk about themselves and their careers, and you want to learn about the career, so ask. Also, think about a person who has mentored you or made an impact on you in the past. Use that relationship as an example of what you are looking for in a new mentor.

Be honest with yourself. Unless you know what help you need and in what areas you need to grow in your professional development, no one can help you.

Gather information. As you talk with your industry experts, gather the answers to some important questions that will help you with your research:

1. What's the best entry-level position in your chosen career?
2. What are realistic salary expectations and job assignments for an entry-level position?
3. What qualities are employers looking for in candidates?
4. Which employers in your desired industry are hiring?
5. Which employers in your desired industry best match your goals?
6. How flexible are your needs? Can you work night shifts? Can you relocate?

As you learn from others, you will also learn a great deal about yourself and what really interests you. Be a careful observer of what does and does not appeal to you, and create a journal or file in which to document what you learn.

NOW HIRING
APPLY
WITHIN

Learn About the Companies in Your Field

Once you understand the general field, it's time to do some formal research on the companies in your field in your area. Many new job seekers make the mistake of plastering the world with their resumes, with little regard for the companies they're actually approaching. It's much better to do the research first and then start your job search. This means finding out which companies you want to work for and what makes those companies unique or special. Learn the names of the people who run the companies or do the hiring. Check out their products, their recent news, and even their competitors. Although this might seem like a lot of work, it won't go unnoticed. Hiring managers appreciate a carefully considered and prepared job application, and they're much more likely to call back an applicant who seems to understand the organization.

The campus library is a terrific resource for your research. You can use the online databases to get information that is not generally available on the Internet, and you can consult reference books, local periodicals, and other resources. Your local public library will also have many useful references.

Start with the companies listed by your local experts (instructors, staff, mentors). This will give you practice in researching companies. After you have done a few, you will have some questions—and those are great questions to ask your local experts, enabling you to strengthen those relationships.

As you search company websites, you are likely to first see the marketing section of the website, where the company talks about its products and services. The language is likely to be optimistic and have a sales emphasis. After you understand the products and services, hunt beyond these sections of the website and read the "About" sections and "Investor" sections, where the company talks about itself and its leadership and shares recent press items about itself. A scan of search engines like Google, Bing, and Yahoo! should also yield useful information.

When you are gathering information about companies, keep careful notes. The job search is a marathon, not a sprint, and you are likely to look back at this information many weeks later. Organize it carefully so that you will be able to remember what you were thinking when you first did the research.

Job Search **Tip**

Use a checklist so that you can compare companies as you learn about them:

- ☐ Company name
- ☐ Corporate parent (Is it part of a larger company?)
- ☐ Ownership/Leadership (Try the "About" part of the website.)
- ☐ Size of the company
- ☐ Key services or products, and how your role would fit in
- ☐ Recent news or press (Who are the competitors? What challenges are there?)
- ☐ Relevant information pertaining to your particular position

Finding Your Ideal Job

The best place to start your job search is online, usually by checking the following resources:

CareerBuilder.com®. Like Monster (listed below), CareerBuilder is a large, national job search engine. CareerBuilder also allows you to narrowly target your job search to specific regions, industries, companies, and salary levels. You can post your resume on CareerBuilder, sign up for alerts, and access the site's tips on job searching and resume building.

Craigslist.org. Craigslist® is a national site that posts classified ads, including job listings. You can search job listings by city and also by industry.

Indeed.com. Indeed.com is an aggregator, meaning that it reposts job information from a wide variety of sources, including newspaper classifieds, company websites, job boards, and other places on the Internet.

LinkedIn.com. LinkedIn® is a popular social networking site for business people. It's a place where you can post a resume and make contacts without sharing your personal information. However, many people don't know that LinkedIn also has local job postings.

LinkUp.com. LinkUp® posts jobs from company websites, including small, medium, and large companies. The postings are automatically updated whenever the company updates its website.

Monster.com®. Monster is one of the largest job search engines on the Internet, with job postings from all over the country. You can tailor your search in a number of ways, including by salary, industry, geography, experience level,

Practice
Critical Thinking

Human resource departments that advertise online often receive hundreds of applications for every opening they post, so it's very important to make sure you stand out from the competition. What are some things you can do to make yourself stand out in a positive way?

and other parameters. However, Monster offers more than classified ads. You can also post your resume, read job search tips, and access additional resources on the site, such as information about companies.

SimplyHired.com. SimplyHired® posts job information from a wide variety of sources, including company sites, job boards, and classified ads.

Analyzing Sources of Leads

So, how are you going to find your 300 job leads? There are actually several types of job lead:

Cold leads. A **cold lead** is a job that is publicly posted and for which you have no connection to the organization. For example, if you go to HotJobs.com and you see a job listing for a job in your desired field in your desired city, but you don't know anybody who works at that organization, then it is a cold job lead. You can also find cold leads in newspaper classified ads, college career offices, career association websites or offices, and many other online and offline locations.

Warm leads. A **warm lead** is a job that is publicly posted, just like cold leads, but in this case you know someone who works at that organization. The person you know doesn't need to be the person who is hiring for the role (or even in the same department).

Networked leads. A **networked lead** is a job that is not publicly posted. The job may

not really be open yet, or the organization may just be thinking about bringing someone in. The reason you know about the job is that someone in the organization told you about it.

Externship leads. Externship leads are leads that come as a result of an unpaid externship that is part of an academic program. The student may be working required hours at a clinical site or may be performing a required externship as part of his or her program.

Purchased leads. Purchased leads are leads that are controlled by someone else. For example, a temp agency or headhunter may have access to a lead for a job that may not be publicly posted. In this case, the candidate or the employer usually needs to pay a fee to the agency if the candidate is hired.

What is the best kind of job lead? The answer is that you are going to need a mixture of leads in your successful job search. The chart below shows the characteristics of the lead types.

Type	Best Place to Find	Difficulty Finding Lead	Chance of Getting Job
Cold	Internet	Easy	Low
Warm	Internet	Medium	Low
Networked	Friends/Colleagues	Hard	High
Externship	School	Medium	High
Purchased	Agencies/Headhunters	Varies	Varies

Maximizing Internet Leads

People tend to spend a lot of time searching for job leads on Internet job boards like Monster.com, because it is very easy to find job leads there and because it is easy to narrow the search by geography, by job type, and even by keyword or salary. However, Internet job leads can also be frustrating because the probability of getting a job from an Internet job lead is low—everyone else can find the same job lead just as easily, so the potential employer is going to get a lot of resumes and cover letters. It will be difficult to stand out. A warm lead is a little bit better because you can call your contact at the company and ask if it's possible to mention you to the hiring manager. This can help you stand out from a pile of resumes (every little bit helps).

Make a wizard. In order to maximize the efficiency of your Internet search, make a list of sites that work well for you, and create an **assistant** or **job search wizard** on each site. This is an automated way of checking whether a job has posted that meets your criteria. Even if the assistant doesn't send you anything, you should still check the site, since you may not have chosen the exact language that the recruiter did in posting the job.

Create bookmarks. Bookmark your job lead sites. You're going to want to go back again and again and again. Remember, searching for a job takes commitment and time.

Be creative in your searches. Try every variation of a keyword until you figure out what recruiters typically write in their posts. For example, try Medical Assistant, Medical Assisting, Healthcare, Health Care, Health Assistant—keep trying until you discover the words that are most common for posts in your area. Your campus instructors and staff may have suggestions that can help, too.

Be determined. Don't try just one site; try every site you can find that seems relevant. Remember, you need a *whole lot* of job leads in order to make your search successful. Look in as many places as you can imagine.

Job Search **Tip**

Don't become too attached to any one particular company or job. You may find one company that's really exciting, and it's okay to get excited, but remember that rejection is part of the personal sales game. You may lose some before you get the job you love. Even if you find a great job or have a great interview, keep looking and keep interviewing. No matter how great your interview was, your search isn't over until you have a signed offer letter.

Job Fairs

Plenty of people still find work through newspaper ads and other offline sources. In fact, newspaper ads are often the best place to find part-time or local jobs; some local companies avoid the big online job search engines because they don't want to get swamped with resumes from across the country. Other traditional sources for want ads include professional journals and trade magazines.

Beyond the want ads, there are a number of ways to look for work without ever turning on a computer. One of the most popular methods is to attend **job fairs,** also known as career fairs. These events are designed to bring together employers and prospective candidates. They are typically advertised ahead of time in local newspapers, on radio stations, on television, and online. If you are uncertain where to find a local job fair, search online for the keywords "job fair" and your city or location.

Job fairs are often targeted at particular types of employees—for instance, college students, health care workers, construction workers, or women in the workforce.

The idea of attending a job fair can be intimidating. They are often crowded and noisy, with people lined up for brief face-to-face meetings with company representatives. It can seem like riding the roller coaster at a theme park: an hour of waiting for one minute of adrenaline and activity. And it can be scary to think about what it will take to distinguish yourself among the crowds of people.

Job Search **Tip**

A job fair can be an excellent opportunity to polish your interviewing skills. Instead of sending out resumes and waiting to be contacted, attending a job fair guarantees that you'll be able to speak to company representatives on the spot. Consider attending a job fair even if your dream employer is not participating in the fair. Start with employers that you are less interested in, and use this as an opportunity to practice answering standard interview questions.

But people find work at job fairs all the time—and you can too. Here are some tips for a successful job fair experience:

- Bring multiple copies of your resume, paper and pens, and business cards if you have them. The whole point of a job fair is to get your information into the hands of hiring companies, so make sure you're prepared.
- Dress professionally, but wear comfortable shoes. You'll want to project a professional aura, but keep in mind that you'll probably be on your feet for a long time, so make sure you're wearing shoes that won't blister your feet or ruin your disposition.

- Prepare a one-minute **elevator pitch.** At a typical job fair, one minute might be all the time you get. So, imagine you're in an elevator with a hiring representative from the company of your choice, and you have only that elevator ride to convince him or her to hire you. Practice this speech prior to the job fair until you have it memorized and can deliver it comfortably and flawlessly.
- Be assertive. Sure, the crowds can be intimidating, but the only way to get noticed is to be in the right place to get noticed. But don't be rude, pushy, or angry. Job fairs can be long, exhausting ordeals, filled with tension and nerves. Never let your sour mood show. Present yourself as an enthusiastic, friendly person with goals.

Networked Job Leads

How can you get a job without grinding through 300 job leads? The vast majority of jobs come from networking, not through online job searches (most jobs are never posted online). Also, employees who found their jobs through networking tend to be more satisfied with their jobs, so start building a network now.

Networking is nothing more than developing positive relationships with people in your related field. Why do you want a network? What can these contacts do for you? A lot. People who are already working in your new career are the first to hear about job openings. They often know about openings before they are posted to the public, and if you are recommended by someone the company already trusts, you can get a real advantage. Contacts in your network can distinguish you from the other people applying for the same job.

A lot of people find the idea of networking intimidating, but you can do it. Just think of it as making friends and building professional relationships.

Here are some tips to get you started:

Use the network you already have! Your family, friends, high school classmates, former coworkers, and neighbors are all part of your network. Spread the word that you are looking to speak with people who may be able to offer you advice. Set up meetings. Always ask every contact for two or three more people he or she can recommend that you speak with. "Do you know two other people who could give me advice about the health-

TrueStory

"I had just graduated from a film program and one of my classmates got this amazing job. He couldn't stop talking about it, so I asked him if the company had any more jobs. He recommended me, and I got an awesome job there, too. Networking is definitely the way to go."

care industry? May I use your name when I contact them?"

Seek advice. Don't ask your contacts for a job; they know you're looking for a job. Always lead with the request for advice. The job opportunities will arise in those conversations as you are seeking advice. It may seem hard to believe, but it really does work that way.

Be interested in others.

This is the easiest trick in the book for connecting with people and making a good impression. It's been said of many successful people that their secret is in making the person they are speaking to feel as if that person is the only one in the room. That's how focused they are on the person! So when you are interacting with people, be interested. Ask questions.

Follow through. Always take the time to meet new contacts face to face. Follow up with a handwritten thank-you note or a formal email. Make sure you stay in touch every month or two to keep your contacts updated on your search and on your meetings with the contacts they referred you to. Check in with your contacts just to say hello.

Join professional associations. There are professional associations that you can join now—as a student—to start meeting people in your field. The time to start building your network is *not* when you are looking for a job. Rather, the time to start building it is *now*, when you can just show up and be interested. That way, several months from now when you are looking for a job in a related field, you will feel more comfortable and you will already have the relationships established that will help you get a job. To meet people, volunteer for committees or help with events and special projects.

Form study groups. Classmates are wonderful additions to your network of contacts. A great way to deepen your relationships with your classmates is to form study groups, particularly if you are a shy person—it's a great way to break the ice and get to know other people. You can even study together online or over a social network. You never know who other people know. Someone you are about to go to school with could introduce you to your next boss. But you'll never know that if you don't take the time to build the relationship.

Your network is one of the most important things you'll need in your career, so start building it now. If you feel as if starting your career is a solitary endeavor, just like studying, you are wrong. It's not. Contacts get jobs. You have to build a network of contacts so you can request information, assistance, and so on. Check your ego at the door.

Externship Job Leads

An **externship** that is part of your educational program is a terrific way to develop a relationship with a potential employer. Externships typically have a very high externship-to-hire ratio. Even if your externship doesn't turn into a job offer, you are most likely gaining high-quality work experience. The supervisors and co-workers at your externship site are excellent networking contacts, since they all work in your chosen field. An externship is a good investment of your time, and you should do as many of them as you can.

You can also offer your services to a company that you like—free of charge—to try to develop a relationship. In most cases, unless you do so as part of a sanctioned academic program, the employer must pay you at least minimum wage, which may discourage employers from taking you up on the offer. However, some employers may be thrilled to give you a try, and there is no better way to send the message that you are willing to invest yourself in a company than to offer your services with the conviction that they will see how great you are on their team.

Employment Agencies and Headhunters

Employment agencies, search firms, and headhunters are professionals or companies that help people find work. There are, however, differences in the way they operate.

Employment agencies are companies that typically fill low- to mid-level jobs. Some employment agencies charge the job seeker, while others are paid by the company. In general, most job search experts recommend against paying an employment agency to help you find work. There are too many ways to find work on your own to justify paying someone else to help.

Like employment agencies, search firms are companies that help people find work. Search firms differ in the way they are paid. Some are paid only when their candidate is hired by a company. These kinds of firms often collect huge databases of resumes and send large numbers of them to companies in need of new employees. It's a good idea to file your resume with search firms that specialize in your target industry.

A second kind of search firm typically aims at higher-level jobs. These search firms are known as "retainer firms," and they are hired by companies to fill executive-level positions. Retainer firms are often hired to fill specific positions, and they are typically paid a percentage of the position's salary, whether or not they fill the position.

Finally, the term **headhunter** is used to describe an employment specialist who helps people find new jobs. Headhunters often work for search firms. The best headhunters are like career coaches—they can help position you to get the best jobs, negotiate salaries, and alert you to new possibilities in your industry. Often, headhunters specialize in particular industries and become intimately acquainted with the companies and people in their business specialty.

Temporary Agencies

A **temporary agency,** or temp agency, is a company that fills short-term positions, often office jobs. Some temp agencies also specialize in the trades and can help fill temporary openings in skilled trades such as HVAC, carpentry, and plumbing.

Companies call upon temp agencies for a variety of reasons. A permanent employee may have gone on an extended medical leave or on maternity leave. Perhaps the company has a major project that must get done or is experiencing a one-time surge in business that requires extra help.

Temp work can be a path to full-time work. Some companies use temp agencies to find permanent employees through "temp-to-perm" positions. However, the hiring company must pay a very large fee to the temp agency in order to hire the temp full-time, so there is a strong disincentive to hiring temps. You are better off doing the hard work up front to land a full-time position.

A Final Tip

As you look for a job, remember to be resourceful and persistent. This means preparing yourself beforehand, using all the tools available, doing research into your chosen industry and local companies, staying organized, and networking with people who already work at the job you want.

KAPLAN success STORY

Eugene Chavarria
Midland, Texas

Attended: Kaplan College—Midland
Area of study: Medical Assistant graduate

I was working at my job and dealing with a patient. She really liked my bedside manner and gave me her card. She was the Director of Nursing at the local hospital. She told me that if I was ever looking for a job to stop in and ask for her. This came in handy when I was laid off a month later. I went in and asked for her and had an interview for the next day! It just goes to show you that you never know who you may meet. Treat every patient or customer with the utmost respect and you may just open a door.

Unit Summary

- Before you start sending out resumes, think about your goals and target the kind of company that interests you.

- Online job search engines are powerful tools, allowing you to locate thousands of job openings and narrowly tailor your search to include only those that are most relevant.

- Classifieds and ads in trade journals are excellent resources.

- Networking is a great way to learn about openings that may not be posted on job sites or in the classifieds.

- Temp agencies, employment agencies, and job fairs are other resources to consider when you are looking for a job.

TO-DO List

✔ Check out all the major **job search** engines. Bookmark and create a **wizard** at each one you use.

✔ Research major professional and trade organizations in your industry. Find out how you can join.

✔ Try to make five new career contacts every week and expand your career network.

✔ Visit the library to see which trade magazines and journals in your field are available there.

✔ Research upcoming local **job fairs,** and write down the dates, times, and places. Make preparations to attend.

✔ Research local employment agencies. Call a few to see if they're a good fit for you.

✔ Create a system for keeping track of all the jobs that you have applied for. Document the name of the company, the position you applied for, the date you applied, and the name of the person you contacted. Save copies of your resumes, cover letters, and applications as you submit them.

Important Terms

How well do you know these terms? Look them up in the glossary if you need help remembering them.

lead

cold lead

networked lead

headhunter

externship

job search wizard

job fair

temporary agency

warm lead

elevator pitch

Online Resources

Job Hunting Tips and Links
JobSearch.About.com

Links to Employers, State Agencies, Classified Ads, and Job Hunting Resources
www.job-hunt.org

The Art of Career and Job-Search Networking
www.quintcareers.com/networking.html

Exercises

1. Create an online profile that you can post to various job search engines.

2. Visit all the major job search engines and create a list of the strengths and weaknesses of each, including which features they offer and how customizable their search is.

3. List ten people you would like to include in your career network, and write a short paragraph describing how you might reach two of those people and form a connection.

Resumes

Organizing your resume so it is clear and clean

Communicating the value of your education and work experience

Highlighting transferable skills from your previous experience

Customizing your resume to specific job descriptions

What are the most important 30 seconds of your life? You could answer this question many ways, but you might consider one critical 30-second interval that you will never see . . . the half-minute when a recruiter reads your resume. A typical big-company recruiter reads hundreds of resumes a day. As part of the job, the recruiter must quickly determine whether your resume is worth a longer read or is not even worth considering. Your resume will probably be reviewed for about 30 seconds, and you will never get a second chance with that recruiter. So, this unit is all about how to make a terrific first impression, so your resume will get a second look.

Marketing Yourself

As you assemble your information and prepare for your job search, you're doing a very important task: you're building your brand. In Unit 6 we will teach you how to create and protect your personal brand—which is the collection of all the ideas you stand for (in a professional sense)—and we will examine the tools you can use to reinforce that brand. The most important tool of all will be your resume.

As you embark on your job search, it's time to start spreading the word about your own brand. In other words, it's time to start marketing yourself. The idea behind a successful job search is to convince a prospective employer that you have the EDGE, that you have the perfect blend of education, skills, experience, and professionalism to excel at the job you're trying to land. If you want to work as a plumber, this might mean you have attended a trade school or served as an apprentice, you are familiar with the newest plumbing-related products on the market, you understand local building codes, and you're enthusiastic and excited about plumbing.

Often, your resume is the first thing a potential employer sees, making it your first chance to communicate who you are. To make a great first impression, you must carefully present every element of your skills and experience to show yourself in the best light. You want the prospective employer to understand that you have all of the necessary skills for the job and that you are also Empowered, Dependable, Goal-Oriented, and Engaged.

Your resume communicates in four key areas:

Your education. Education is a primary means of validating that you have learned the critical knowledge and skills in your field. Although there are still occupations that can be obtained with a high school diploma or GED, these are increasingly rare. More and more companies require some form of higher education as a stepping stone into the workplace. The minimum requirement may be a diploma, an associate's degree, a bachelor's degree, or an advanced degree. Make sure to showcase all of your relevant educational qualifications on your resume. Even if you haven't finished your educational program yet, you can still show the employer the skills that are taught in your program and what you are expected to achieve by graduation.

Your skills. Whether you're promoting yourself to an employer through your experience or your education, you want to show that you have the skills necessary to perform the job you desire. Not all employers require direct job experience; many employers expect to train employees on the job after they are hired. Part of marketing yourself is identifying valuable skills you already have, called **transferable skills,** and then showing how they relate to the job you want. For example, if you're hoping to work in the front office of a medical clinic, your experience as a hostess in a restaurant might show that you have the necessary people skills to deal with patients. Always look for ways you can relate your past skills to your present job aspirations, even if they don't seem obvious.

Your extracurricular activities. Just as colleges and universities seek well-rounded applicants, employers often like to know that their prospective employees are active. It's especially helpful if you're a member of one or more organizations related to your chosen career. An example is membership in a woodworking club or society if you want to work in carpentry. You can also use positive travel experiences, such as field trips, to reinforce your appeal. For example, any conventions or seminars you've attended in association with your chosen career should be listed on your resume. The idea is to demonstrate your enthusiasm by showing that you continue to pursue your career, even when you are off the clock.

Practice
Critical Thinking

Make a list of your skills and experiences. Which of them do you think are most appealing to your target employers? How can you highlight these most effectively?

Volunteerism. A history of volunteering or donating your time in the service of others is always a good thing. In addition, the skills you developed working as a volunteer can be listed on your resume. If you've given a significant amount of time to nonprofits or to an organization such as the American Cancer Society, make sure a potential employer knows about it (especially if it's related to your career). Just be careful to avoid political or religious discussions during a job interview.

Standing Out in a Competitive Job Market

The job market is always competitive, but some job markets are especially difficult, and some roles are more challenging to win than others. You must always assume that the person who is reading your resume is tired, busy, overwhelmed, and impatient. You may be surprised to know that you cannot assume that the resume reader knows a great deal about the details of your career—sometimes resumes are screened by recruiters who have been trained in human resources or even as executive assistants—so your reader may be a generalist who does not understand industry jargon. Your resume reader is probably giving each resume just a brief glance and then making a decision about whether to put it in the "Definitely Read" pile, the "Maybe Read" pile, or the "Definitely Not" pile.

Stay out of the Trash Can

Your first goal should be to stay out of the "Definitely Not" pile. Your resume will end up in the outbox or even the trash can if it falls into one of a few categories:

Has spelling or grammatical errors.
When you communicate on IM (instant messaging), on SMS (texting), or on social networks like Facebook and Twitter, you may be used to using abbreviations, using all lowercase letters, or letting the occasional spelling error go. Prospective employers will not be so kind. The person reading your resume knows nothing about you, so if you cannot go to the trouble to remove spelling and grammatical errors from your resume, the prospective employer is likely to conclude that you will not go to the trouble to follow up on important details on the job. Use a computer spell checker, and then have at least two people check your final resume for spelling errors. There's no way to recover from a poor first impression.

Appears too "cute" or is otherwise unprofessional. Clip art, borders, graphics, and other designs look great on invitations and gift cards, but they do not belong on resumes. Also, stay away from fancy paper, colored paper, colored ink, and perfumes. Use standard paper and a regular laser printer. If your resume stands out as unprofessional in appearance, it will be tossed immediately. (There is one exception here: If your career field is graphic design, digital art, or another artistic area such as event planning, you may be expected to demonstrate your style on your resume; consult a trusted professional for guidance as to the range that is considered professional.)

Doesn't match required qualifications. If the job posting says "CPR Certification required" and you don't have "CPR Certified" on your resume, you're going in the "Definitely Not" pile. You really do need to have the qualifications in the job posting listed on your resume. Candidates seem to assume that it can't hurt their cause to just apply anyway, even if they don't fit the qualifications, but it can irritate a recruiter if you apply when you do not have the proper credentials. Doing so may hurt your chances at any future role at that organization, especially if you have an unusual or memorable name. Think twice before sending off a resume when you can't meet the qualifications.

Doesn't follow instructions. If the job posting says "no more than 500 words," you're taking your chances by going with 510. No kidding. Don't end up in the trash can

> **True**Story
>
> "I am a Vice President of Marketing, and I get resumes all the time that have sloppy formatting, spelling errors, and nutty sentences. Seriously? I can't give you a marketing job if you can't even market yourself!"

because you were tripped up by simple instructions. Many employers introduce instructions in the job search process just to see whether you can follow them. Such employers assume that if you won't follow instructions on your resume, you also won't follow critical instructions on the job.

Has errors that are critical to the role.
If you are applying for a job as a grammar teacher, you'd better not have grammatical errors on your resume. If you are applying for a job as a proofreader, there had better not be typos, misspellings, or style errors on your resume. Your resume will go straight to the trash can if you make an error in an area that the reader finds ironic.

Get into the "Yes" Stack
Staying out of the trash can is a good thing, but your odds of getting an interview and an offer are still less than 1 percent if your resume ends up in the "Maybe Read" pile. If you can get into the "Definitely Read" pile, your odds of getting an interview can jump dramatically. You need to be one of the top five choices to have a reasonable shot at an interview. Here are some tips for getting your resume into the "Yes" stack:

Match the job qualifications exactly.
Tailor your resume (or your cover letter, which we will discuss in Unit 5) to exactly match the job posting. Use the language in the job posting, and show how you have exactly the knowledge, skills, and experience required. If there is an area in which you do not have exactly the required skill, include the most similar skills you have that are transferable.

Know the company.
Read the organization's website to see what's important to them. Companies use specific language to refer to the equipment and processes that are most important to them. You can adopt their language to describe your experience in your resume.

Eliminate irrelevant material.
Don't pad your resume with irrelevant information. You're better off leaving the resume clearer (and easier to read) with exactly the right information that matches the desired job.

Think like a scanner.
Large companies often use scanners to filter through large stacks of resumes. The scanner uses optical character recognition technology to hunt for keywords in your resume. So, it helps to know a company's likely keywords and insert them in your resume. As you research the industry and the company, keep a list of possible keywords. You can use them on your resume, in your cover letter, and in your interviews.

Get help from an insider.
People who work at the organization know the culture there and are the best source of information about what hiring managers want. If you can find someone who works at the company and who is willing to read your resume and provide advice, you will have the best possible probability of getting into the "Yes" stack.

SCENARIO

You're fine-tuning your resume to apply for a job that looks exactly right for you. You really want to maximize your chances on this one. What should you do?

QUICK FIX: Even if you don't know anyone at the company, there are still a lot of things you can do to help your cause. Try to figure out the company's important "buzzwords" or keywords. Go to the company's website and look in the Press section; or Google the company, look under News, and read every article in that area. If you read the company's websites, all of the press about the company, and everything you can find on Google, you can make a good guess about what keywords are important to the company. Put them on your resume, in your cover letter, and in your interview preparation.

Selecting Your Resume Format

Your resume should be in a standard format so that it appears professional. You can acquire a standard format from the Career Services staff at your Kaplan Higher Education campus, from Optimal Resume (see box), or from a number of other sources. We do not recommend the resume templates provided with Microsoft Word, because they often give candidates considerable trouble (they can be difficult to format and do not scan well).

Here are some important guidelines for resume format:

Make it chronological. A **chronological resume** is arranged by time (most recent job on top, the job before that one below, and so on). Employers like to be able to clearly see what has happened over time. If you have a lot of experience, you need to cover only the last ten years or the last three to four jobs, whichever is longer. You may see some **functional resumes** (organized by grouping skills together, independent of time). This can work well for candidates who have large gaps in their employment history or who are changing careers. The downside of this approach is that employers tend to be suspicious of it, thinking that you are trying to hide something, and they will just reconstruct the timeline themselves or ask you to do it (or, worse, just throw your resume away and read one that is easier to read). You are better off making your resume chronological and explaining the gaps in your career up front.

Keep it to one page. The only reason to go to two pages is if you are applying for an executive role and you need to convey the depth of your management and operational experience. If you make the reader go to a second page, it had better be worth it! If you don't have at least ten years' work experience or an advanced degree, definitely keep it to one page. If you do go to a second page, make sure your name and a page number are on the second page, or it may be lost.

Margins 0.7 inch, font 11-point Times New Roman. Unless the job posting specifies margins and fonts, there will be no dire consequences for slight differences (for example, a 1-inch margin is a little large, but still all right; 10-point font is really too small, but 12-point is probably okay; Arial is a reasonable, conservative font). Your name should be in a larger font for emphasis (anywhere from 14- to 18-point is good, and boldface is fine).

Use formatting to emphasize key points. Bullet points are easy to read, so list your accomplishments under each job with simple bullet points. You can use boldface to highlight key points, but only do so once or twice—bold print everywhere will look unprofessional.

Spell words out instead of abbreviating or using acronyms. You cannot assume that your reader understands your industry lingo. If you think that the abbreviation or acronym could be a keyword, definitely

Optimal Resume

Optimal Resume is an online tool that will help you build your resume, cover letter, and portfolio—and it can even help you prepare for your interview. To get started, go to https://kheu.optimalresume.com and click on "Create a New Account." All you need to do to launch your account is use your email address provided by your Kaplan Higher Education campus.

include it—just follow it afterward with an explanation in parentheses. Example: ER (Emergency Room).

Make high-quality hard copies. Print your resume on high-quality, white, letter-size (8-1/2" × 11") paper, using a laser printer. Print on only one side. Print several copies, so you can carry some hard-copy resumes to your interviews. Do not fold or staple your resume when you send a hard copy.

Putting It Together

So, let's start at the top. Your resume should include:

- Contact Information
- Summary
- Education
- Work Experience

You do not need to include "References available on request." The employer will assume this to be true. You can leave negative issues off the resume. If the employer inquires in an application or interview, you can deal at that time with issues such as a criminal record. You should not list salary history on your resume (we will discuss salary further in Unit 9). Also, you should avoid listing personal information such as political and/or religious beliefs and hobbies, unless you believe that they will be relevant for the employer.

Contact Information

Your contact information must include your full name, phone number, and email address. Remember, the email address needs to be your name and should not include any cute personal words or phrases. It is considered professional to include your physical ("snail mail") address, as well. If you do not include a physical address, the employer may find it unusual, which could diminish the impression of professionalism.

Summary

Some resumes include an objective. This is a standard element, but it turns off some employers, who consider it redundant. (After all, every applicant's objective is to get a job!) It is safer, therefore, to put a simple summary statement at the top of the resume, giving the employer a one- to three-sentence summary of what makes you an attractive employee. Example:

> Medical Assistant with strong understanding of medical care procedures, patient education, and health insurance billing. Excellent problem-solving skills and attention to detail. Efficient in patient interaction and time management.

> Information technology professional with experience in supporting software and hardware systems. Background includes installing, configuring, modifying, and troubleshooting Windows operating systems and software, as well as experience in determining, planning, acquiring, and implementing systems to track client information.

Education

Since you will be applying for jobs immediately after completing an education program, it makes sense to put your Education section toward the top of your resume (right below the Summary). This placement highlights the recent growth in your knowledge and skills. This can be especially helpful if you have no work experience or if you are changing careers. If your education is merely the next step in a standard career progression and you have great work experience, you may choose to reverse the order and put your Work Experience section above your Education section.

The Education section should include:

- Your current program (marked "Expected graduation date: [fill in the date]")
- Any previously *completed* degrees (possibly including your high school diploma or GED)
- Professional certifications by *recognized* organizations
- Languages in which you are *fluent* (Expect to be tested in the interview if you claim to be fluent.)
- Whether you are a U.S. permanent resident (Include this information only if you believe it is relevant.)

Work Experience

Start with your most recent job at the top of the Work Experience section. For each entry, list the name of the company or organization, your job title there, and the city and state in which you were based for your position (not where the company is based). You also need to include the month and year when you started and ended each role at the company or organization. You should follow this information with a one- or two-sentence summary of your role. After this summary, provide brief bullet points to display your accomplishments, skills, and experiences. For example:

Perry Police Department   **Perry, Iowa**

Externship   January 2011–March 2011

Observed police officers and department staff as they performed their regular duties and responded to unusual and emergency situations. Performed entry-level administrative tasks when assigned by supervising officer.

- Observed police officers taking control of a criminal offender.
- Assisted in creating files for criminal offenders, according to department procedure.
- Accompanied police officers in rides around Perry's jurisdiction on various shifts.
- Participated in new-officer training sessions, including ethical behavior training and conflict resolution.
- Performed entry-level dispatch computer tasks, such as running car licenses and looking up case files.

When possible, show accomplishments, not duties. Show that you not only performed your job, but also helped the organization reach its goals. Describe something that you achieved, if you can. This is not always possible, especially if your job was at the entry level and did not involve a great deal of decision-making authority, but do your best to list accomplishments. Here are some things to think about as you assemble the Work Experience section of your resume:

Demonstrate measurable results. If you really want to impress a prospective employer, fill your resume with change statements (accomplishment, strategy, results). First, you describe a change that you made at the organization, followed by the strategy you used to make that change. *Make sure to describe your results with dollars, numbers, or percentages.* For example, "Transformed a struggling construction site into an efficient operation by creating an inventorying system that saved the company $10,000 in two months." Here's another example: "Reduced crime in District 72 by 14% by instituting a gang rehabilitation program that cut violent crimes by 32 in a one-month period." Again, this can be difficult if your role was an externship, as in the resume example above. If you did not have the opportunity to create change, describe what you did do and list the skills that you used. However, if you were able to create change, get it onto your resume!

Show progress over time. If you have a history of being promoted quickly, make sure that's really clear on your resume. Employers are wary of employees who sit in the same job for a long time or who hop from company to company after one or two years without making any progress. If you can demonstrate progress on your resume, it will really help you stand out.

Explain gaps. Rather than leaving a gap in your resume, explain what you were doing, as gracefully as possible. If you were doing anything valuable (even if unpaid) during that time, insert it into your Work Experience. Examples:

1995–2000	Maternity leave and family development
1995–2000	Full-time parent
1995–2000	Supporting an elderly parent
1995–2000	Parenting, plus community service

Highlight desirable personality traits. Our research shows that employers favor employees who are Empowered, Dependable, Goal-Oriented, and Engaged. Think about your work experience. Can you find examples that demonstrate that you are poised, that you present yourself well, that you are punctual, that you are dependable? Have you ever won a school award for attendance or a work award for dependability, such as Employee of the Month? Think of what you have done that shows initiative, leadership, confidence, and the ability to think of what needs to be done before you are asked. What have you done that shows you are good on teams, a real team player? Now, include these items in your bullet points. You want employers to know that you are the kind of professional that they want on their teams.

Include only what is relevant. Try to think like a prospective employer. If you were hiring, you wouldn't want to know every little thing about the prospective employee. You would only want to know the important things. So, for example, if you are going to list your skills, list only the ones that are relevant to the job. Don't list every single skill you have. If you are listing computer skills, list the ones that are really likely to matter on that job.

Frequently Asked Questions

Here are some answers to questions that are frequently asked about resume writing:

What if I don't know exactly what kind of job I want? This is common, especially at the beginning of the job search. Just write a different resume for each type of job, and label them so you can keep them straight. You will tailor each resume to the specific position anyhow, so it makes sense to keep a few different types. It is much better to tailor your resume to the specific posting than to send a generic resume.

What if I don't have any work experience? You probably have some relevant volunteer work in the past that you don't think of as important. Talk to a family member or friend to brainstorm, and you may be surprised by what comes up. Even if you've got absolutely no work experience, there is still time to build some experience.

There may be an externship as part of your program. If so, it is an especially valuable resume builder. Pay careful attention to the skills you are learning, and make sure they all get onto your resume. Be aggressive in networking to find a place that will let you do some volunteer work right away. Even a month or two of volunteer work can make a big difference on your resume.

What if I have been a job hopper with lots of short-term jobs? The job-hopper image will make employers nervous, so you will want to minimize it. You can group similar jobs into a single line, especially if they were several years in the past. Examples:

1995–2000	Teaching (Johnson Elementary, Jackson Middle School, Hampton Elementary)
1995–2000	Restaurant Work (waiter, short-order cook, busboy, bartender)

If a job is unimportant to the overall story of your resume or occurred a long time in the past, you can eliminate it.

What if my title didn't really explain what I did? If your official job title doesn't really describe what you did, you can use the official title and then follow it with the better description. Example: Administrative Assistant (Office Manager).

Avoiding Common Resume Errors

Writing a good resume is tough, but it's easy to write a bad one!

Here are some common errors to avoid as you are putting together the most important tool in your personal sales arsenal:

Don't be your own proofreader. Modern technology is wonderful, but don't rely on the spell checker alone to proofread your resume. After you use the spell checker, you should have at least two people who are not familiar with your resume proofread it and give you feedback. They may catch spelling, grammar, and style errors. They will also be able to tell you if anything doesn't make sense or doesn't flow well. Don't become angry with your proofreaders—they are your best source of objective information! If they see something undesirable in your resume, you had better pay attention to it, because a recruiter is likely to have the same reaction.

Don't bore your reader. Great resumes use strong verbs. Use past tense for things you accomplished in the past (achieved, acquired, launched) and present tense for accomplishments on your current job, if applicable (collaborate, lead, develop). Here is a great list of verbs to help you as you are writing:

achieved	conducted	expanded	minimized	recruited
acquired	constructed	explained	motivated	reorganized
adapted	contracted	forecasted	negotiated	researched
addressed	convened	formed	obtained	resolved
administered	created	founded	operated	responded
analyzed	demonstrated	generated	organized	reviewed
anticipated	designed	guided	originated	selected
assembled	developed	hired	oversaw	separated
assisted	devised	implemented	performed	simplified
audited	doubled	improved	planned	solved
budgeted	drafted	informed	prevented	staffed
calculated	edited	interpreted	produced	started
centralized	eliminated	interviewed	programmed	supervised
changed	enforced	launched	promoted	surveyed
collaborated	ensured	maintained	provided	tested
composed	established	managed	publicized	trained
condensed	evaluated	marketed	published	used

Don't use weak titles. Weak titles are vague and generic (such as "Nursing"); strong titles are specific (such as "Pediatric Night Shift Nurse"). If you use weak titles, the employer will pass right by your resume, and you won't end up in the "Definitely Read" pile.

Don't use *I, my,* **or** *me.* Everyone knows that the resume is all about you. It reads strangely to have first-person pronouns in a resume. Find a way to rephrase the sentence so that you do not use *I, my,* or *me.*

Don't repeat yourself. Avoid using the same words or phrases over and over.

TrueStory

"When I was 18, I really wanted this job, so I lied on my resume about having a degree. When I was 45, I was the victim in a very serious car accident, and the attorney for the other side found out that I had lied on my resume all those years ago. I couldn't get a settlement because they said they couldn't calculate my lost wages. They assumed that if I lied on my resume, I must have been lying now. I had no idea that lying on my resume could have such serious consequences."

Don't lie on your resume. You may feel tempted to exaggerate your accomplishments, especially if you feel as if you do not have enough experience to win a job that you really want. The goal is to describe your achievements clearly, so that the prospective employer has a clear picture of what you can do. It will not serve either of you if you get in over your head. Avoid self-flattering terms such as "highly skilled," "outstanding," or "excellent," since these do not typically read well to an objective reader. Be honest, but not too modest. But never, ever lie. First, your integrity should be important to you. Second, employers today are diligent in their research, and there is a high probability that you will be caught. Third, even if you get away with it, lying on your resume could have very serious consequences later in your career that you cannot even imagine today.

Resume Analysis

One of the best ways to become an expert resume builder is to analyze other people's resumes. Here is a great checklist to use for resume analysis:

General Impression
- [ ] Format is neat
- [ ] Paper is standard, high-quality, letter size, white, laser-printed
- [ ] Format is consistent
- [ ] No spelling, grammatical, or style errors
- [ ] Job titles are specific and eye-catching
- [ ] Verbs are strong and describe achievements
- [ ] No use of *I, my,* or *me*
- [ ] No repetition of words or phrases
- [ ] No confusing language
- [ ] No "cute" graphics or colors

Contact Information
- [ ] Full name, phone number, email address, and "snail mail" address

Summary
- [ ] One- to three-sentence summary of what makes the writer an attractive employee

Education
- [ ] Current program (marked "Expected graduation date: [fill in the date]")
- [ ] Any previously *completed* degrees (possibly including high school diploma or GED)

- [ ] Professional certifications by *recognized* organizations
- [ ] Languages in which the writer is *fluent*

Work Experience
For each job, starting with most recent on top:

- [ ] Name of the company or organization
- [ ] Job title(s) there
- [ ] City and state in which employee was based
- [ ] One- to two-sentence summary of role
- [ ] Brief bullet points to display accomplishments, skills, and experiences
- [ ] Accomplishments, not duties, if at all possible
- [ ] Measurements of results (dollars, numbers, and percentages), if at all possible
- [ ] Demonstrates that the employee helped the company or organization reach its goals
- [ ] Highlights that the employee has desirable traits such as poise, confidence, punctuality, dependability, leadership, teamwork
- [ ] Shows that the employee has been steadily promoted over time
- [ ] Explains gaps and shows that the employee can keep a steady job
- [ ] Includes what is relevant and does not include irrelevant information

STEVEN WEEKS

123 Rosewood Avenue Penbrook, PA 34511
555-555-5555   steven@optimalresume.com

OBJECTIVE

Seeking a position as a medical assistant in a fast-paced environment where helping people with their health care needs is a top priority. Adept in both clinical and administrative settings.

EDUCATION

Kaplan Career Institute, Harrisburg, PA	10/2010–7/2011
Registered Medical Assistant	10/2010
American Red Cross	11/2010
Certified Nursing Assistant	1/2007

RELATED EXPERIENCE

Dewey, Fixem & Howe, Internal Medicine Harrisburg, PA   1/2007–Present
Certified Nursing Assistant

- Assist patients with bathing, dressing, hygiene, and grooming in accordance with established care plan.
- Obtain specimens, weights, and vital signs of patients.
- Assist doctors and nurses with examinations and procedures.
- Provide pre-operative and post-operative patient care and monitoring.
- Sterilize and maintain bio-medical equipment.
- Support doctors, nurses, and other staff by filing, charting, and documenting.
- Perform billing and coding tasks, create referrals, and schedule appointments.
- Manage supply inventory.
- Take incoming calls and messages while running front desk.

Home Care Providers of Colonial Park Colonial Park, PA   2/2005–1/2007
Receptionist

- Answered phones and greeted customers; directed calls to the appropriate designations.
- Demonstrated superb communication skills, both verbal and written.
- Sorted and forwarded mail.
- Performed various errands for doctors and nurses.
- Assisted with infants and toddlers in the lobby.

VOLUNTEER ACTIVITIES

Volunteer, Habitat for Humanity

Volunteer, Race for the Cure Fund Raiser, United Way

Figure 3.1 Chronological resume

Lisa Hart

123 Rosewood Avenue
Detroit, Michigan 48201
555-555-5555
lisa@optimalresume.com

CAREER OBJECTIVE

Professional position in accounting or finance

PROFESSIONAL SKILLS PROFILE

One year of related work experience, plus an internship, in combination with strong academic training and credentials in:

- Accounts Payable & Accounts Receivable
- General Ledger & Cash Reconciliation
- Credit & Collections Operations
- Corporate Banking & Asset Leasing
- Financial Analysis & Reporting
- Economic & Demographic Analysis
- Budget & Cost Analysis
- Project & Team Leadership

EDUCATION

Associate's degree – Business Administration, 2010
Kaplan College, Detroit, Michigan
Honors & Activities:

- President, Student Accounting Club
- Member of the Society for Financial Professionals

EMPLOYMENT EXPERIENCE

Bookkeeping Assistant   September 2008 to present

TCI TECH SOLUTIONS, INC.

Flint, Michigan

Part-time permanent staff position with one of the region's fastest-growing telecommunications companies. One of the first three employees hired into the Accounting and Finance Department, which currently employs more than 25. Instrumental in creating accounting systems and procedures to support the company's accelerated growth and nationwide expansion. Earned four promotions in three years.

- Assisted the CFO with designing and automating the company's accounting, financial reporting, cash management, banking, and leasing systems.
- Wrote and produced a 200-page accounting procedures manual.
- Coordinated software upgrades and enhancements with internal IT staff.

Accounting Intern   Summer 2008

GRAYSTONE FINANCIAL SERVICES, INC.

Dearborn, Michigan

Full-time summer position with a financial and accounting services firm. Worked in cooperation with professional staff to prepare journal entries, maintain general ledgers, reconcile bank statements, and prepare financial reports for clients in the transportation, telecommunications, and hospitality industries.

Waitress/Hostess   Summers 2006 and 2007

THE TOWNE MARKETPLACE

Flint, Michigan

Fast-paced customer service position in one of the area's finest restaurants and resorts. Gained excellent experience in public relations, special events planning, and cash handling/reconciliation.

Figure 3.2 Functional resume

Jonathan "Jon" Doe

5555 5th Street Des Moines, Iowa 50055
515-555-5555 JonDoe@yahoo.com

Office Manager and **customer service** professional with diversified experience. Highly qualified in service-based positions requiring an emphasis on customer satisfaction in a fast-paced environment. Strong rapport with personnel, customers, and associates based on knowledge, professionalism, and integrity.

Skills Summary

Scheduling	Problem Solving	Creative Talent
Software Applications	Planning / Scheduling	Computer Literacy
Continuous Improvement	Deadline Dependent	Task Completion
Expediting Solutions	Time Management	Conflict Resolution

Education

Kaplan University, Des Moines, Iowa and Mason City, Iowa

Associate of Applied Science Degree in Business Administration   July 2011–December 2011
  • Concentration in Management

North Iowa Area Community College, Mason City, Iowa

Associate of Arts Degree in Liberal Arts and Sciences   August 1997–May 1999

Employment

Kinfolks Texas Style BBQ, Altoona, Iowa

Assistant Manager   May 2007–Present
  • Supervise and lead back-of-the-house and assist in front-of-the house training.
  • Order food products and inventory; perform weekly, monthly and quarterly inventory.
  • Coach, train and develop line cooks, servers and additional staff.
  • Monitor day-to-day operations to ensure compliance with established standards of product quality, service and clientele.
  • Open and close the restaurant Successfully interact with customers and other associates.

Old Navy, West Des Moines, Iowa

Store Manager   April 2004–May 2007
  • Handled merchandise placement and presentation.
  • Maintained responsibility for daily operations, banking, loss control, payroll, budgeting, hiring, and staff development for 1.5-million-dollar facility.
  • Supervised 2 assistant managers and 10 other employees. Conducted retail sales staff training sessions.
  • Reviewed sales figures and prepared month, season and year projections.

Assistant Manager   August 2000–April 2004
  • Set responsibilities and goals for selling specialists.
  • Coordinated new groups on selling floor.
  • Skillfully resolved all customer service issues to gain mutual satisfaction.

Panera Bread, Ankeny, Iowa

Certified Trainer/Sales Associate   February 1999–July 2000
  • Completed Certified Trainer Course, learning how to train new associates and how to hold casual instructional and how-to meetings.
  • Operated cash register.
  • Cooked and prepared foods for deli counter.
  • Initiated cleaning and sanitation of food preparation area.

References

Available upon request

Figure 3.3

WES SMITH

333 Lomis Ave   Des Moines, Iowa 50333   (515) 333-3333   wessmith@yahoo.com

OFFICE MANAGER/ADMINISTRATOR

Experience in planning and directing executive-level administrative affairs and support. Combined organizational and communication skills with the ability to independently plan and manage diverse business relationships.

EDUCATION

Kaplan University   Des Moines, Iowa
Bachelor of Science Degree in Management   October 2010–March 2011
Associate of Applied Science Degree in Business Administration   January 2006–September 2010

RELEVANT SKILLS

Marketing: Understanding the relationship between the consumer's needs and wants and the business's effort to be able to supply the demand.

Marketing Management: Analyzing the social forces and the international aspect of marketing and in-depth discussion of the marketing mix.

Research and Presentation: Applying different research methods and effective ways to present information.

Conflict Resolution: Focusing on individual and group interactions in a complex work environment.

WORK EXPERIENCE

Children and Families of Iowa   Des Moines, Iowa
Administrative Assistant Intern   December 2010–March 2011
- Highly organized and effective time manager, good secretarial skills, phone coverage, filing, sorting mail, data entry, activity scheduling, and general office duties.
- Accepted increasing responsibility, demonstrating flexibility and ability to learn quickly.
- Accustomed to fast-paced, high-pressured positions, demonstrating ability to prioritize multiple tasks, meet deadlines, and provide quality service.
- Created and edited newsletters, utilizing a variety of desktop publishing programs.

Real Estate Services Inc.   Ankeny, Iowa
Office Manager   January 2008–February 2010
- Handled all general office duties; filing, answering phones, making appointments, and contacting clients.
- Processed incoming payments and recorded deposits with 100% accuracy.
- Improved the efficiency of existing operational procedures.
- Served as sole administrative liaison to entire staff and all company contacts.
- Compiled large amounts of date and created readable documents.
- Developed and implemented database for tracking production records and expenditures.
- Studied management methods, improved workflow, simplified reporting procedures, and implemented cost reductions.

Administrative Assistant   March 2007–January 2008
- Answered calls, scheduled appointments, entered data, faxed, typed, and made outbound follow-up calls.
- Prioritized work, met conflicting deadlines, and utilized a variety of software programs to produce high-quality work.
- Provided support to management, handled routine administrative work, coordinated statements, maintained records, and tracked information.

Manpower   Des Moines, Iowa
Suspense Processor (CitiGroup)   May 2006–March 2007
- In charge of obtaining necessary information for input into the system (ACAPS).

Figure 3.4

Jacquelyn "Jackie" Jones

222 2nd Avenue P.O. Box 22 Des Moines, Iowa 52222
222-222-2222 Home   222-222-2222 Cell
jjones@gmail.com

Dispatch

Dedicated, proactive law enforcement professional with extensive education and training in the criminal justice field. Outstanding leader with a firm but fair attitude and a reputation for honesty, integrity, and loyalty. Possesses excellent written and verbal communication, documentation, and administration skills.

- Has 120 hours of internship experience with Perry Police Department.
- Observed interviews with principal and eye witnesses. Recorded facts and prepared reports to document.
- Assisted with expedited processing of prisoners and prepared and maintained records of bookings.
- Relayed complaint and emergency-request information to appropriate agency dispatcher.

Education

Kaplan University, Urbandale, Iowa   Expected January 2012
Associate of Applied Science Degree: Criminal Justice
Solid foundation of Criminal Justice and the skills of various specialized employment areas such as law enforcement, corrections and private security.

- **Juvenile Delinquency:** Individual and community systems, as well as the juvenile justice systems and all facets involved in the understanding of how a child's development state and social milieu affect both delinquency prevention and intervention strategies.
- **Criminal Law:** Crime causation to the extent of crime, victimization, social/psychological theories, and various types of criminality, including violent, property, and public order offenses.
- **Criminal Procedures:** Thorough understanding of our justice system from the time of arrest through the sentencing of the criminal offender; victim's rights and effects of gangs on the crime problem.
- **Criminal Evidence:** Constitutional concepts such as the exclusionary rule, search and seizure, confession, and discovery.

Relevant Experience

Perry Police Department, Perry, Iowa   October 2011–December 2011
Internship
- Observed Police Officers taking control of an offender who committed a crime.
- Assisted in the making of an offender's file.
- Accompanied the Police Officers in many rides around Perry's jurisdiction on various shifts.
- Observed many training sessions of a new Police Officer, such as jail school training, many videos on ethnic backgrounds, and how to deal with situations that an officer may come upon.
- Developed sharp observation skills for understanding the dispatch computer, running car licenses, looking up case files, and informing Police Officers of a crime.

Capstone Concentration: Police Operations
- Examine roles, responsibilities, issues, and trends related to contemporary law enforcement organizations.
- In depth coverage of community policing; policing in selected foreign countries; civil liability; extraordinary problems and practices; public expectations; and police careers.
- Constitutional concepts such as the exclusionary rule, search and seizure, confession, and discovery.
- Strong understanding of the justice system from the time of arrest through the sentencing of the criminal offender.

Work History

Bayard Nursing and Rehab, Bayard, Iowa   August 2009–March 2011
Certified Nursing Assistant

Spring Valley Community, Perry, Iowa   May 2007–June 2009
Universal Worker

Figure 3.5

Claudia Smith

7777 Rose Avenue Apt #7 Boston, Massachusetts 57777
(515) 777-7777   csmith@yahoo.com

Bilingual (Spanish/English) criminal justice professional with emphasis in juvenile mentoring. Combined organizational and communication skills with the ability to independently plan and manage diverse business relationships. Strong time management and problem solving skills with ability to set priorities and manage multiple tasks.

Education

Kaplan Career Institute, Boston, Massachusetts
Associate of Applied Science Degree: Criminal Justice   Expected January 2012
Criminal Justice Club Member

Relevant Experience

Fifth District Department of Corrections, Boston, Massachusetts
Facilitator (Contract)   January 2011–Present
- Work with offenders in Day Programming. Facilitate BEP, Batter's Education Program.

Internship   November 2011–January 2012
- Observed offender intake meetings.
- Used the ICON program, a computer program that records information about offenders.
- Shadowed Probation Officer and assisted with disposition meetings, home checks, and offender assessments.
- Demonstrated ability to assess risk with proactive precautions and respond appropriately.
- Assisted the team in potentially violent arrest situations by helping with lockdowns and head Counts.
- Worked with people from various socioeconomic and ethnic backgrounds.
- Gained solid working knowledge of team building and group cohesion under stressful situations.
- Trained in proper pat down searches, in-takes, check-ins and check-outs, and verification of the offender's place of assignment.

Employment History

American Security, Boston, Massachusetts
Guard Check   August 2010–December 2010 and April 2011–Present
- Provide a wide range of security and guard services. Monitor all security equipment, ensuring full functionality.
- Accurately prepare and complete reports, records, logs and related documents.
- Ensure evidence is properly collected, documented and handled.

Sequel Youth Services, Woodward, Massachusetts   November 2009–August 2010
Teacher/Counselor/Mentor (TCM)
- Supervised youth in activities in order to observe or effect changes in their social behavior.
- Maintained the security of the facility and grounds.
- Provided crisis intervention with juveniles.
- Utilized leadership and authority in a consistent manner and in such a way as to reinforce the residential philosophy and program of the academy.
- Collaborated as a member of the staff team in enforcing all regulations and procedures within the guidelines of the overall resident treatment plan.
- Coordinated adolescent Peer Education/Outreach Programs in the community and within educational settings.

Volunteer Work

Polk County Crisis Advocacy, Arlington, Massachusetts   July 2008–Present
- Provide support to Advocate/Counselor, handle routine administrative work, schedule appointments, maintain files, and track information.
- Create fliers, pamphlets and materials for presentations. Schedule appointments, file and copy documents.

ISED Venture, Charleston, Massachusetts   June 2007–September 2007
- Assisted with making copies of the training material. Translated flyers and distributed them among the Latino community.

Figure 3.6

Evan Smith

1111 Idaho Street Des Moines, Iowa 51111
515-111-1111 Evans@aol.com

Help Desk Support
Experience in providing technical assistance to business professionals. Demonstrated ability to integrate computer skills, customer support experience, and related education to exceed technical business and customer requirements.

Skills/Strengths
- Installing, configuring and supporting Microsoft Windows 95, 98, 2000, NT, and XP.
- Gathering information about testing, documenting, and implementing new software and hardware.
- Strong knowledge of network adapters, RAM, hard drives, and dual monitor cards.
- Networking skills, including knowledge of DNS, WINS, DHCP, and TCP/IP.
- Solid organizational, communication, leadership, and customer service skills.
- Professional troubleshooting, problem solving and analytical skills.

Education
Kaplan University, Des Moines, Iowa
Bachelor of Science in Management: Information Systems Concentration   Expected 2012
Associate of Applied Science: Computer Information Systems: Networking   2010–2011

Relevant Contract Experience
Teksystems, Des Moines, Iowa
Desktop Technician—Allied and Farm Bureau (Contract)   2008–Present
- Actively track and follow up on trouble tickets through Magic tracking system.
- Image and install approximately 1,000 new PCs and train users on new software.

Techstar, Des Moines, Iowa
Desktop Technician—Wells Fargo Financial (Contract)   2007–2008
- Built, maintained, and repaired computer systems to improve speed, reliability, and efficiency of operations.
- Provided high-quality, results-driven, prompt, and professional customer service and support, using Remedy Tracking System.
- Migrated computers from Windows 95 and NT to Windows XP and added applications to newly migrated computers.

Employment
Agricredit Acceptance LLC, Johnston, Iowa
Management Processor   2005–Present
Process and fund contracts. Send merge doc letters to customers as well as dealers. Assist dealers and customers with frequently asked questions about funds and contracts.
- Process over 30 contracts on a busy day, getting funding within 24 hours, increasing budget by 5%.
- Posting AV's, a non-cash transaction to GL accounts for the Processing, Leasing and Risk departments.

Customer Service Representative   2003–2005
Handled inbound and outbound calls. Faxed, printed and copied. Created Word documents and letters to be sent to customers and dealers. Tracked current dealer and customer information, using Excel spreadsheets.
- Dealt with more than 100 calls per day, which decreased the call volume by 10%.
- Accurately calculated 1099 for tax purposes.
- Figured manual and variable rate payoffs.

Military Experience
Iowa Army National Guard   2003–Present
United States Marine Corps   1999–2003

Figure 3.7

Kenneth Smith

2222 Vista Dr. Apt. 222   Houston, Texas 52222
(222) 222-2222   (222) 222-2222
Kensmith@gmail.com

SUMMARY OF QUALIFICATIONS

Information technology professional with experience in supporting software and hardware systems. Background includes installing, configuring, modifying, and troubleshooting Windows operating systems and software, as well as experience in determining, planning, acquiring, and implementing systems to track client information.

EDUCATION

Texas School of Business, Houston, Texas   2010–Present
Associate of Applied Science: Network Administration
- Expected Grad Date: November 2011
- Perfect Attendance

SKILLS

Computer and Network Security	Troubleshooting and Problem Solving	Domain Administration
Local Area Networks (LAN)	Proficient in Microsoft (MS) Applications	Active Directory
Network Administration	TCP/IP and Network Communication	Database Management
Wide Area Networks (WAN)	Client Technical Support and Training	PC Hardware Design
Maintenance and Repair	Proficient in Windows Operating Systems	Project Management
Hands-on Technical Leadership	Server Setup, Configuration and Installation	Process Automation

EXPERIENCE

State of Iowa—Department of Inspections and Appeals, Houston, Texas
Information Technology Internship—120 hours   2010
- Installed operating systems and applications.
- Identified and researched problems on workstations and LAN, including IP resolution, cabling problems and peripheral malfunctions.
- Provided maintenance, installation and configuration of network and workstation hardware and software.
- Re-imaged laptops and desktops, and maintained hardware infrastructure.
- Resolved Microsoft desktop application (Word, Excel, Power Point and Outlook) issues.
- Observed routine maintenance and user file backups.
- Provided technical assistance to staff, assisting with network access, printing and application software operation.

Kelly Services, Houston, Texas   2008–2010
Title Clerk Level 3
- Designed new database that provided real-time monitoring of all client activities.
- Performed timely and highly accurate data entry to ensure fastest turnaround possible for HIPPA letters.
- Experimented with new technologies and routines to increase efficiency and reduce processing time.

VOLUNTEER EXPERIENCE

Bud Open
- Scholarship program to help students pay for college

Kids Fest
- A festival for children, sponsored by **Big Brother Big Sister**

Youth Ministry
- Program that works with troubled youth to provide guidance

REFERENCES

Available upon request

Figure 3.8

Laura Smith

777 7ᵗʰ Ave S Apt 7   Altoona, PA 57777   Phone: (515)777–7777   Email: LauraSmith@hotmail.com

Medical Assistant with strong understanding of medical care procedures, patient education, and health insurance billing. Excellent problem-solving skills and detail-oriented. Efficient in patient interaction and time management.

Education

Kaplan College   Pittsburgh, PA
Associate of Applied Science Degree: Medical Assisting   07/2011–01/2012
- Graduated Summa Cum Laude GPA 4.0

Des Moines Area Community College   Boone, IA
Liberal Arts   08/2009–07/2011
- GPA 3.78

Skills & Accomplishments

Patient/Room Preparation	Communication	Physician Assistance
Pregnancy Test	Pharmacology	Medical Coding and Insurance
Medical Office Management	Medical Transcription	Electrocardiogram
Venipuncture	Urinalysis	Blood Work
Strep Tests	Mononucleous Tests	Injections

Externship Experience

Highland Park Family Physicians   Pittsburgh, PA
Medical Assisting Externship—Kaplan College   11/2011–01/2012
- Assisted medical personnel in the planning, evaluation, and delivery of patient care.
- Instructed patients in proper care and helped individuals take steps to improve or maintain health.
- Performed initial assessments, charting, and ordering of lab work as necessary.
- Facilitated and documented care for patients of all ages, from infants to geriatric.
- Provided patient care under the direct responsibility and supervision of a physician.
- Assisted medical staff and physicians in the preparation of physical exams and surgical procedures.
- Assisted in care and treatment of allergy patients and administration of immunizations.
- Conducted quantitative and qualitative analyses of body fluids, such as blood and urine.
- Drew blood from patients, observing principles of asepsis from blood sample.
- Conducted mononucleous tests, urinalysis, and strep tests.

Employment

Coventry Health Care of Pennsylvania   Pittsburgh, PA
Provider Relations Coordinator   06/2008–12/2009
- Coordinated National Provider Identifier (NPI) project.
- Maintained provider demographic information, fee schedules, payment rates, and billing information.
- Reconciled and submitted various monthly reports.

Cahaba Government Benefit Administrators, LLC   Des Moines, IA
Postpay Analyst/Adjudicator   06/2007–02/2008
- Monitored Corrective Actions Plans and Medical Review referrals.
- Set up/removed edits in claims system and QA'd claims to be sure automated edits were working correctly.
- Calculated provider claim overpayments upon review of medical records.

Wellmark Blue Cross Blue Shield   Des Moines, IA
Postpay Analyst/Adjudicator II   08/2006–05/2007
- Calculated provider claim overpayments and adjusted claims.
- Wrote and updated various desk procedures.
- Completed special projects for Medicare and the Regional Office (CMS).
- Participated in several workgroups, one of which created a customer satisfaction survey.

Figure 3.9

Deborah Smith

Home 515-333-3333 Cell 333-333-3333
333 Hillside Ave Towson, Maryland 50333
Deborah333@yahoo.com

MEDICAL ASSISTANT

Health care professional with both clinical knowledge and field experience to assist with patient care. Ability to perform laboratory procedures and receptionist duties. Motivated to obtain professional value by utilizing knowledge and medical experience.

EDUCATIONAL BACKGROUND

TESST College of Technology   Towson, Maryland
Associate of Applied Science Degree in Medical Assisting   September 2009–March 2011
Dean's List   President, Student Senate
Medical Club   Coalition of Diverse Students

CLINICAL AND MEDICAL OFFICE EXPERIENCE

ABC Family Medical Center   Ankeny, Iowa
Medical Externship   October 2007–January 2008

- **Administration**
  Greeted, scheduled and referred patients as appointed by physician. Conducted routine calls to patients.
  Maintained filing system, screened mail-faxes, managed patient file's, did medical coding, transcribed medical documents, and handled reception duties as needed.

- **Laboratory Techniques**
  Collected and prepared specimens for transport to lab and performed urinalysis. Performed pregnancy, strep, and mononucleosis tests. Performed blood chemistry (glucose, cholesterol) and hematology procedures; RBC, WBC and hematocrit. Obtained blood specimens by venipunctures and finger sticks; PT (Pro Time). Performed injections.

- **Exam Room Techniques**
  Roomed patients. Completed vitals on patients (of all ages). Draped patients when needed. Set up for procedures (women's vaginal checks). Placed EKG tabs on patients when ordered by physician.

CERTIFICATION AND TRAINING

CPR   HIPAA   Mandatory Reporting
Certified Student Leadership   Residential Attendant Training   CNA Training

EMPLOYMENT HISTORY

TESST College of Technology   Towson, Maryland
Federal Work Study Program   March 2010–March 2011

- Student Services, College Library, Admissions, Academic Success Center

Intrepid USA Healthcare Services   Urbandale, Iowa
Certified Nursing Assistant (CNA)   January 2006–May 2007

- Met home health care needs for residents in private homes and/or facilities.
- Transported clients to Iowa City, Iowa, for necessary appointments.
- Kept records of clients, documenting medications and daily activities.
- Earned "Employee of the Month" award.

Progress Industry   Johnston, Iowa
Certified Nursing Assistant (CNA)   March 2004–January 2006

- Case Management: Met with potential clients to determine eligibility for care.

Bethpage   Des Moines, Iowa
Nursing Assistant   May 1999–March 2004

- On call to care for approximately 20–30 residents in private homes.
- Recorded daily maintenance and tracked daily use of company vehicles.

Figure 3.10

Lisarae Koch

North Huntingdon, Pennsylvania

Attended: Kaplan Career Institute—ICM Campus, Pittsburgh, Pennsylvania

Area of study: Associate in Specialized Business—Criminal Justice

If you take one thing away from this course, it should be this: Always remember you will be judged by your resume. Take pride when putting it together and keep it updated in a portfolio.

Kaplan made it possible for a single mother of two, in her 40s, to not only go to school, but to stay in school. The instructors and administration go above and beyond the call of duty. I also found career planning to be a valuable class in addition to my criminal justice classes.

Unit Summary

- Resumes need to be individually tailored for targeted jobs so that it is immediately obvious to a prospective employer that the job seeker is a good fit for the company and its culture.

- Be certain your resume is free of all typographical, grammatical, and formatting errors.

- All resumes should include contact information, a summary, education information, and work experience information.

TO-DO List

✔ Prepare a personal file at your desk or on your computer where you can keep all the information about your employment history and educational experience so that it is handy to refer to as you build your resume.

✔ Critique a variety of sample resumes from online sources, this book, or your classmates. What do these resumes do well?

✔ Compile a list of keywords that are specific to your field, and start using them now.

Important Terms

How well do you know these terms? Look them up in the glossary if you need help remembering them.

chronological resume

functional resume

transferable skills

Online Resources

Online Resume Writing Tool
https://kheu.optimalresume.com

Resume Writing Tips and Sample Resumes
http://career-advice.monster.com/resumes-cover-letters/careers.aspx

Resume Tips on QuintCareers.com
www.quintcareers.com/resume-dos-donts.html

Exercises

Write your answers on a separate piece of paper.

1. Use the Resume Analysis checklist to analyze two or three of the sample resumes in this book. How could you help each job seeker improve his or her resume?

2. Use the same critical eye as you did for resume analysis, and write a quick rough draft of your own resume. Start thinking about your resume right away. Remember, it is your best tool for marketing yourself!

3. For the purposes of this exercise, imagine a specific job you'd like to apply for at a specific company or organization. Adapt your resume for this target. What keywords might be important at this company or organization?

UNIT
4

Portfolios

Using a checklist to ensure that you include all standard elements

Identifying additional elements that will help you stand out

Collecting the documents that will go into your portfolio

Organizing your portfolio in a way that will show a future employer what you've done and what you hope to accomplish

Assembling your portfolio

ou might think that only "creative types" such as graphic artists or journalists use professional portfolios, but in reality, a well-constructed portfolio can help almost any job seeker, in almost any career. A great portfolio can signal to an employer that you have the EDGE. When you hand over your portfolio to a prospective employer, you're instantly accomplishing a few key goals:

- Showing off your organizational skills by presenting a professional, comprehensive, well-organized portfolio
- Demonstrating your skills by providing samples of your work
- Indicating that you are serious about your career and are willing to take the time to develop a portfolio that highlights your achievements

This unit examines what should be in your portfolio and provides some tips on how it can be used to your best advantage.

What Is a Portfolio?

A **portfolio** is a snapshot of your professional accomplishments. It differs from a resume in a couple of important aspects:

- It is much more in-depth than a single sheet listing your work experience; unlike a resume that shows what you *have* done, a portfolio gives an employer an idea of what you *can* do.
- It allows you to "show, not tell." Your resume outlines your skills; your portfolio backs up your resume by *showing* your skills.

Your portfolio can include any document or work sample that might be important to prospective employers. Examples include certificates of achievement, samples of your work, awards, **letters of recommendation,** and anything else that helps provide a complete picture of you as a person and an employee.

If you think of your resume as a snapshot of your skills, then you should think of your portfolio as the feature-length movie.

What Goes in a Portfolio?

Throughout your life, you've no doubt received many certificates of recognition and accomplished things of which you were proud. There might be trophies or awards from sports in which you're involved, scholarship letters, papers of which you're especially proud, letters of recommendation, and on and on. So how do you know which parts to include in your portfolio?

Here's the simple answer: think of your portfolio as a story. It's not a random collection of documents, but a cohesive binder that tells a **narrative,** or story. More specifically, it shows how you've grown academically and professionally, what you're capable of, where you're heading, and why you belong in your chosen career.

Once you start thinking of your portfolio in these professional terms, it will become easier to decide which pieces to include. Maybe your Little League certificate of achievement doesn't belong after all—unless you're aiming for a coaching position.

Components of Your Portfolio

Although your portfolio should be specialized for your industry, there are certain elements that belong in any portfolio. Don't worry if you're still a student or don't have a wealth of professional work samples. Your portfolio isn't meant to illustrate only what you've done; it should show what you're capable of doing in the future.

Your portfolio should contain the following components:

Title page and introduction. This simple sheet should introduce you and contain a simple, brief statement of your professional goals. Your goals should be broad, not tailored for any particular interview. In other words, your goal shouldn't be, "Land this job," but "Establish a long-term career in the [blank] industry, ultimately rising to [blank] position."

Your resume. This is not a substitute for handing over your resume, but your portfolio should include a copy of your current resume.

Contact information. Some portfolios include areas for business cards with contact information.

Samples of your work. This can include everything from coursework to published articles to artwork.

Degrees and certifications. Include degrees and certifications that you've earned and a description of any relevant coursework. You may also want to include your transcripts.

Awards and honors. This can include any honors or awards you've received for your coursework or outside activities, positive performance evaluations from your workplace, and perfect attendance certificates from classes.

Reference list. A sheet of references should direct prospective employers to people who can vouch for your work habits and skills. If you have letters of recommendation, include them in this section.

Matching Your Industry

Obviously, the portfolio of a graphic designer will look dramatically different from the portfolio of a dental assistant—but both individuals can benefit from having a portfolio. The following list gives examples of documents that professionals in a variety of industries can include in their portfolios.

Business program graduates. White papers, reports, advertising campaigns, promotional ideas and documents, cover letters, brochures, marketing campaigns, presentation outlines or slides, case studies, memberships in professional organizations

Criminal justice professionals. Research projects and presentations, mock trial projects, fingerprinting work, field experience internships, crime scene work and photographs, memberships in professional organizations

Allied health professionals. Certificates of training, sample patient records (use fictitious patients to protect patient privacy), HIPAA certificate, research project on diseases and drug intervention, treatment protocols, adult and infant CPR certification, transcription reports, memberships in professional organizations

Graphic artists. Transcripts, sample projects, published work, letters of recommendation, group projects, multimedia projects, fine art projects, illustrations

Office administration/management professionals. Speed certificates for typing, certificates for note taking, samples of penmanship, attendance records from school, sample business communication, presentations including slide shows and PowerPoint presentations

Writers. Writing samples from a variety of media, awards, multimedia projects, research projects

ON THE JOB

SCENARIO: You are at your first job interview after graduation, and things are going very well. You're a little bit nervous, but you've easily handled some tough questions. Suddenly the interviewer asks you a simple question about what you liked best about your coursework, and for some reason you draw a blank. You reply that you liked writing best of all, but you struggle to complete your thought.

QUICK FIX: Since you have your portfolio on hand, you offer to show the interviewer an example of your writing. You direct her to the section in your portfolio that has your technical writing samples, and as she looks through the samples, you use the slight pause to regroup. Because you are so familiar with your portfolio, you feel confident talking about your writing samples. Your nerves are back under control, and you use your writing samples as a starting point for discussing your unique strengths as a technical writer.

This list is just to stimulate your thinking, but as you can see, the options are almost endless. In essence, anything that shows mastery of your field or highlights skills you've developed that relate to your industry belongs in your portfolio. Additionally, personal recognition and testaments to your character—such as records of volunteer work, blood drive certificates, and evidence of community recognition—can help a prospective employer better understand what kind of person you are.

Gathering Your Documents

For many people, one of the most challenging aspects of assembling a portfolio is gathering the material. Faced with the prospect of job hunting, they launch a mad hunt to find the proper paperwork, assemble it, and pull together a portfolio. While you can build a portfolio this way, you'll almost certainly end up with a better product with some advance planning.

As you progress through your coursework, you should keep a special folder or box titled "Portfolio." This is where you'll put documents that will someday be candidates for your portfolio. For example, if you produce an especially good report for a class, immediately place this in your portfolio folder. You can also get portfolio material from your outside activities. For example, a certificate of recognition from an organization where you volunteer could also be included.

When it comes time to assemble your portfolio, you will review all the material and then decide what stays and what goes. Remember, not every piece of paper you collect will actually make it into your portfolio. But it's better to have too much to work with than too little, so don't hesitate to build a large collection of prospective documents for your portfolio.

Assembling Your Portfolio

Your portfolio is a physical document—the way it looks and feels can say almost as much about you as what's inside it. It's essential that your portfolio is neatly and professionally organized, is free from simple spelling and grammar errors, and contains only your best work.

Here are some tips for organizing your portfolio:

1. Use an attractive three-ring binder or, better, a leather portfolio case. The actual binder will vary depending on your paperwork—artists have larger portfolios to accommodate their drawings—but choose the very best you can afford. (Don't worry—a prospective employer will not expect to keep your portfolio, only review and return it.)

2. Use tabs to separate sections and chapters. Colored tabs, with a matching table of contents, will help employers quickly navigate through your portfolio. You can organize sections according to their content, using such headers as Research Projects, Resume, Awards and Recognition, Education, Letters of Recommendation, Volunteer Work, Slide Shows, References, and so forth.

3. Use the highest quality paper and backing material you can. Every document in your portfolio should be individually and professionally presented. Don't simply throw a bunch of article clippings or drawings in a folder; instead, mount them on individual pages. If you're presenting reports and longer items, make it easy for the reviewer to access the information. Remove staples and tape.

4. If you cut out articles or sections from reports, use scissors and obtain a clean margin. Don't include anything that looks ragged, stained, or worn. If your certificate of achievement is stained, don't include the actual certificate, only a mention that you received it.

5. Make sure your contact information is current. Every email address, website, and phone number in your portfolio needs to be current at all times. Double-check these before you use the portfolio, and update them if necessary.

Your Portfolio Online

A basic paper portfolio is still a great resource, but if you really want to set yourself apart, consider creating a simple online presence that works in conjunction with your portfolio. It's fairly easy to build a simple website by using an off-the-shelf template from a web hosting company such as Yahoo! or GoDaddy. Creating a simple website requires reserving your web address, designing the site, and paying for hosting services (usually about $50 a year, at the minimum).

If you choose to build an online companion to your portfolio, make sure to provide the website address in your portfolio and on your resume and business cards. The Internet can help you only if people visit your site.

Optimal Portfolio

The resume-building website Optimal Resume offers a portfolio builder that allows you to easily create an online portfolio. You can organize your portfolio by section and upload documents to include in each section. The site supports a variety of file types, including document, image, and video files. When your portfolio is complete, it can be shared online or downloaded as a compressed file. Visit https://kheu.optimalresume.com to get started.

Using Your Portfolio

Your portfolio is a tool that presents you in the best possible light. It shows employers your past accomplishments and gives them a well-rounded view of you as a person as well as an understanding of your professional goals. The best portfolios tell a story about you as a person and an employee and make it easy to understand why you would make a great employee.

Your portfolio can be a powerful tool during the job interview process, and there are certain steps you can take to maximize its impact. First, you should always take your portfolio with you to job interviews. At the interview, you can present the portfolio to your interviewer at the appropriate time. However, don't expect the interviewer to sit and absorb your entire portfolio during the course of the interview. You can use it during the interview to direct the interviewer to pages as you answer questions and discuss your background.

If you hand the portfolio to your interviewer after the interview, make sure either to include a request that the portfolio be mailed back or to offer to stop by and pick it up. It's widely understood that portfolios are not meant to be kept by employers—portfolios often require significant investments of time and money to produce, so it's not reasonable to expect a prospective employee to leave a portfolio behind.

Unit Summary

- Your portfolio is a collection of documents that gives a detailed history of your accomplishments and an idea of your future goals and direction.

- Include in your portfolio certificates of achievement, transcripts, letters of recommendation, projects, and work samples that give a complete picture of your skills.

- Your portfolio should be matched to your career and include supporting documents that would interest and engage professionals in your field.

- You can also include documents that show your character, such as records of volunteer work, community recognition awards, and letters of reference.

- Use your portfolio during an interview to provide examples of your qualifications, or leave it for the interviewer to review, with arrangements to collect it later.

- An online presence, such as a website, can be a powerful tool to help boost your portfolio.

TO-DO List

✔ Brainstorm a list of all possible documents that will go into your **portfolio.** Don't worry about organizing the list. The goal is to have a large number of possibilities that you can refine later.

✔ Obtain a box or a folder that you can use to store the documents that will go in your portfolio.

✔ Buy the portfolio materials so you'll have them on hand when you put together your portfolio.

✔ Make a list of ten people you can ask for a **letter of recommendation.**

Important Terms

How well do you know these terms? Look them up in the glossary if you need help remembering them.

letter of recommendation   portfolio   narrative

Online Resources

How to Use a Portfolio in an Interview
www.jobweb.com/interviews.aspx?id=342

Benefits of Maintaining a Career Portfolio and a Current Resume
www.jobbankusa.com/CareerArticles/Resume/ca93005a.html

Portfolios: The Art of Finding a Job
http://alis.alberta.ca/ep/eps/tips/tips.html?EK=151

Exercises

Write your answers on a separate piece of paper.

1. Plan the organization of your portfolio. What skills are most important in your field? What sections should your portfolio include to highlight these skills? Create a table of contents for your portfolio, listing each section.

2. For each section in your portfolio, make a list of documents that you'll need to include in the portfolio. Your list should include documents that you already have and a plan for additional documents to include as you complete your coursework.

Tillie Shearer
East Chicago, Indiana

Attended: Kaplan College—Hammond
Area of study: Massage Therapy graduate

A portfolio shows all of your accomplishments in one place. I have all of my certifications from all of my modalities in Massage Therapy. This is very important so employers know you can work on each body part. I keep my proof of insurance and all of my academic awards. Scholar awards are given every quarter so this is a great highlight along with my transcript. I have my professional membership card (ABMP), my national certification (NCBTMB), a copy of my CPR card, and of course my diploma and resume! It really looks nice and professional to show a potential employer!

Cover Letters
and Applications

Writing a cover letter that highlights your greatest strengths

Tailoring your cover letter to the exact job description

Customizing your cover letter to make your application stand out

Filling out your job application clearly

When you realize how important a resume is—and that a typical reader will look at it for less than a minute—you may start wishing that the resume could talk! How are you going to get across to the recruiter how amazing you would be for the job in only one 30-second glance? Fortunately, most recruiters will take the time to read a cover letter—if it is brief, clear, and well written. The cover letter gives you a golden opportunity to make yourself stand out. In this unit, you will learn how to use the cover letter to give yourself an advantage.

Cover Letters

When you are competing for a job with many other qualified candidates, you need a way to differentiate yourself, to make your application stand out from the rest. The cover letter presents an excellent opportunity to differentiate yourself from competing candidates. The cover letter is a terrific way to convey to the prospective employer that you have the EDGE qualities (Empowered, Dependable, Goal-Oriented, Engaged). Employers expect to see the following elements in a **cover letter:**

- The date, your name, and the position for which you are applying
- Your contact information, located clearly at the top or bottom of the letter
- Clear, precise language, with no grammatical errors

- An explanation of why you are interested in the position and the organization
- A description of why you would be a good choice for the position

The cover letter should be brief—never longer than one page—with short paragraphs. Remember, your reader is very busy and is reading a lot of letters and resumes; you want to make the job easier, not harder.

Format

Because the cover letter and resume are all that the potential employer can see at first, they represent your only opportunity to demonstrate professionalism before being contacted for an

---

619 S. Smith Dr.
Michigan City, IN 46360

August 1, 2011

Mrs. Susan Clark
Human Resource Department
Parsons Widgets
450 South St.
Michigan City, IN 46360

Dear Mrs. Clark:

    Please find my resume enclosed, in response to the Production Assistant position posted on Monster.com. As a recent graduate of Kaplan College's Associate Degree in Business Administration program, I am well prepared for this role. Also, as a lifetime resident of Michigan City, I grew up with Parsons Widgets as a household name in electronics, and I would be very excited to join the Parsons team.

    This past summer, at Hartz Technologies, I served as an intern in production and performed the duties listed in your Production Assistant position, including process design, process management, and reporting. My supervisor, Mr. Morgan, has graciously volunteered to serve as a reference so that you can verify that I am a hard worker, a team player, and a capable production assistant.

    Please do not hesitate to contact me at (313) 555-1212 if you have any questions. I am available at your convenience for a personal interview. Thank you in advance for your time and consideration.

Sincerely,

Janice Garza

Enclosure: resume

Figure 5.1 Cover letter

interview. So, demonstrate that you know how to write a standard business letter. Note in Figure 5.1 that the candidate's address is first, followed by the employer's name, title, and address. The salutation is followed by a colon, which signals that the letter is a formal letter. (Commas are considered informal.) The letter includes the name of the position, the location of the posting, and the critical information described above. Note that even though the candidate's phone number is on the resume, it is also in the letter, so the employer will not have to shuffle pages in order to call. Also, the candidate's name is typed at the bottom, so the employer can read it clearly even if the signature is not legible.

If your cover letter will be sent electronically, you may not have a choice about how it is formatted. If you have to submit it in a web-based form, it is best to remove all bullet points and other formatting marks (use line breaks instead of bullets, for clarity). This will increase the chances that the letter will format clearly on the other side. If you can add your letter as an email attachment, then the best thing to do is to turn it into a PDF, which is a document that is an image that cannot be edited. If you have Adobe Acrobat, it's easy to do this: Just print the document from your word-processing program, and choose "Adobe PDF" as your printer instead of your regular printer. Save the document in the same folder as the original document, and be sure to attach the PDF version to the email. This will ensure that your cover letter comes out just the way you want it to look.

Content

The letter in Figure 5.1 is a standard cover letter, but it is not going to make the candidate stand out. If you don't know anything about the employer, you won't get into trouble with a standard cover letter. You can try to develop some networking contacts in the company and stand out that way. However, if you are a strong writer, you may choose to take a chance and write a more striking letter. Figure 5.2, on page 70, is an adaptation of a real letter that was sent to high schools by a recent college graduate who wanted to get a job as a high school teacher in a very difficult job market.

The strategy in this second cover letter is very different. The writer surprises the reader in the first sentence. The reader is expecting the same old sentence that every other candidate has written—something to the effect of "All I've ever wanted to be my whole life is a teacher." However, the writer turns it around and makes it a little surprising. This cover letter was unique, and it attracted the attention of employers and got the candidate several very interesting interviews. You do need to be careful in writing an unusual cover letter, since what you think is funny or unusual may come across very poorly to an employer. So, if you want to try this strategy, just make sure to try out your letter on some trusted professionals before you send it.

Cover Letter **Tips**

- Your cover letter should cover the points in the job description and explain how you are qualified for them. Don't be afraid to use a bulleted or numbered list if it helps you make your point clearly.

- Don't copy your resume exactly in your cover letter, but do highlight your greatest strengths. Ask yourself, "Why should this company want to hire me?" Then make sure your letter discusses those reasons.

- Make sure to say something specific (and complimentary) about the company. You want the recruiter to know that you have done your research and you really know the company.

- Make sure to sign your letter. Don't use pencil or an unusual color—black or blue ink is considered professional.

1211 Orange Grove Blvd.
Pasadena, CA 91105

May 1, 2010

Mr. Don Jackson
Dean of Faculty
Montrose School
225 N. Magnolia Ave.
South Pasadena, CA 91108

Dear Mr. Jackson:

When I was a child and people asked me what I wanted to be when I grew up, my answer was always the same: a fireman! I could just imagine running into burning buildings and helping people and riding on trucks and carrying ladders. Today, many years later, and having just completed my bachelor's degree, I have discovered to my surprise that I really want to be a teacher instead. It's really not a lot different in a lot of ways. I still want to help people, but I'll be carrying books instead of ladders.

I had the great privilege this past summer of participating in the summer teaching fellows program at Northbridge School in Connecticut. I taught a summer course in expository writing under the supervision of a terrific master teacher, and I had an opportunity to practice classroom management, work my way through some early mistakes, and build my curriculum for a full-time English teaching position. I was terribly excited when I saw your job listing. I attended Montrose School in grades 7–9 and have very fond memories, especially of Mrs. Morgenstein, who taught me World Geography and retired last year.

I do feel that I have a special understanding of Montrose experience and have a great deal to give back, both to the students and to the faculty team. I would look forward to discussing this with you in person at your convenience. Please do not hesitate to contact me at (313) 555-1212 if you have any questions. Thank you in advance for your time and consideration.

Sincerely,
Mark Jarvis

Enclosure: resume

Figure 5.2 Cover letter

Applications

Hiring processes vary, so be prepared to be flexible. Some employers will ask you to take a written test or practicum. Some employers will interview you one-on-one, while others may have several people in the room at the same time. Some organizations like to have you come in for one interview at a time, while others will have you meet with several people in the same day. You may be tempted to try to guess how things are going, but try not to read too much into the process. Just present yourself well, and use the process as an opportunity to learn.

Most employers will ask you to fill out an **application** at some point in their process. It may be before you come in to interview, at the site when you come in to interview, or after the interview. It may seem that the application just asks you for the same information you have on your resume, but in a different format. That is typical. Just keep your resume handy as a guide, and fill out everything on the application, even if it means copying directly from the resume. The application may require more information than the resume, so when you arrive for your interview, it is always good to bring additional information, including the following: driver's license, Social Security card, contact information for references and previous employers, your previous addresses (up to five), and your starting and ending salaries for each of your last jobs (up to five).

Use the following guidelines when filling out an application:

- If you can, photocopy the application and write your rough draft on the photocopy.
- Do not use pencil or an unusual color of ink— black or blue ink is considered professional.
- Follow all the instructions carefully—the employer may be testing your attention to detail.
- Make sure job titles and dates exactly match your resume—again, this shows your attention to detail.
- Answer all questions—if something does not apply to you, write "N/A" for "not applicable."
- If the form asks for a desired salary range, write "negotiable"—never provide a range, which could limit your chances.
- If the form requests a reason for voluntarily leaving a previous job, write "new opportunity"—never write anything negative about a previous employer.

> ### **True**Story
>
> "I was scheduled to interview a candidate, and he called me from the airport and said he couldn't get through airport security and couldn't come until the next day. I told him to just go home. If he couldn't figure out how to get to the interview, what was he going to be like on the job?"

- When you are finished, review everything and then copy the information neatly onto the final application form.

Attention to Detail

When you reply to a job posting, follow all the instructions. Employers think through their job processes very carefully, and if they put something into a job posting, they mean it. If the posting says that you must be able to speak French, be prepared to speak French in your interview. If the posting says that your cover letter must be no more than 500 words, don't make it 520 words. It may not seem like much to you, but if you can't follow instructions during the job search process, the employer may conclude that you won't follow instructions on the job. You are competing against many other capable, trained individuals. If you want to win the job, you need to display top-level professionalism. The superior professional pays attention to every detail and is very careful in the submission of the cover letter and application.

ON THE JOB

SCENARIO: Your last boss was a tyrant, and you hated him, which is why you left your job. The application form asks why you left your job. You want to be honest, but you're not supposed to write anything negative. What should you do?

QUICK FIX: Everyone understands that some bosses are unreasonable, but it won't help your cause to write this on an application. The new employer doesn't know you and may assume that you are difficult to manage or a complainer. So, instead of focusing on why you left, focus on where you would like to go and write something positive, like "I wanted a role with more opportunity to develop my leadership skills."

Lisa Diane Arnett
Pittsburgh, Pennsylvania

Attended: Kaplan Career Institute—ICM Campus,
Pittsburgh, Pennsylvania
Area of study: Business Administration—Management
Employer: School Management Assistant, Board of Education

If you take one thing away from this course, it should be this: To know more, you must stay open to learning more!

Kaplan was very instrumental in preparing me for the work force. They strengthened my weak areas in writing and interviewing and gave me the confidence I needed to apply for jobs that I would have otherwise bypassed due to inexperience.

KAPLAN
success
STORY

Unit Summary

- A cover letter should accompany every resume you send.

- The cover letter should expand on skills that are covered in your resume.

- Neatness counts: make sure your cover letter is error-free.

- In addition to sending a resume and cover letter, expect to be asked to fill out a job application.

- Before sending your resume and cover letter to a prospective employer, make sure you know the employer's preference for receiving them. Should materials be submitted via email or uploaded through the company's website? Follow instructions very carefully, because employers are testing your attention to detail.

TO-DO List

✔ Prepare a personal file at your desk or on your computer where you can keep all the information about your employment history and educational experience, so that it is handy to refer to as you complete **cover letters** and job **applications.**

✔ Critique a variety of sample cover letters from online sources, books, or classmates. What do they do well?

Important Terms

How well do you know these terms? Look them up in the glossary if you need help remembering them.

cover letter

application

Online Resources

Online Cover Letter Writing Tool
https://kheu.optimalresume.com

Cover Letter Writing Tips and Sample Cover Letters
http://career-advice.monster.com/resumes-cover-letters/cover-letter-samples/jobs.aspx

Exercises

Write your answers on a separate piece of paper.

1. Create a rough draft of a standard cover letter that you can adapt to target specific positions.

2. For the purposes of this exercise, imagine a specific job you'd like to apply for at a specific company. Adapt your cover letter for this target.

3. Try a creative opening for your cover letter. Do you think it will improve your chances?

Personal Brand

hat do you want people to think about when they think about you?
Your sense of humor? Your designer wardrobe? Your tattoos? Your
compassion and intelligence? Your answer to this question is more important
to finding the right job than you might think, because it concerns your
personal brand. If you feel that you don't have a personal brand, then it's
time to develop one. This unit will help you identify and develop the elements
of your personal brand.

What Is a Brand?

A brand is a series of ideas, impressions, and feelings that you hold about a particular product, company, or person. We are surrounded by brands, and companies spend thousands or even millions of dollars each year on marketing that is designed to create and strengthen our brand impressions.

Brands have power. A customer who holds a favorable impression of a brand may choose that product over another, even when the chosen brand has a higher price than a very similar alternative. For example, two detergents may have essentially the same ingredients, but a customer may choose the more familiar brand, even if it is more expensive. Why would a customer do something that seems so irrational? Customers choose brands that they trust—once they have had a positive experience with a certain brand, they remember that positive impression and are more likely to return to that brand in the future.

The most important thing about a brand is the perceptions that customers hold about it.

A brand can include several kinds of ideas:

Adjectives. What are the words that the brand brings to mind: *strength, power, cool, calm, savvy, smart?* Think of a list of keywords or adjectives. These are key brand elements.

Emotions. How does the brand make you feel: energetic, fun, playful, hip? Pinpoint your feelings. These are also key brand elements.

Values. What do you believe about the brand: ethical, environmental, counterculture, cool? The last part of the brand picture is your **perception** of the values that are associated with the brand. For example, if the company donates a percentage of all proceeds to saving the environment, then you will probably perceive the brand to be "green" or "eco-friendly."

It takes a long time to build a great brand. The strongest brands—like Coca-Cola®, McDonald's®, and IBM®—are many decades old. Unfortunately, it does not take long to destroy a brand. Think how quickly you would stop eating a food product if you heard that it was making people sick. How long would it take you to go back to a skin lotion if you heard that it blistered some people's skin? It doesn't take much to do a lot of damage to a good brand.

> ## Practice
> ## Critical Thinking
>
> Think about your favorite type of car. What do you like about this brand of car? Where do you picture yourself driving it? What feelings and impressions does it create? Write down the elements of your favorite car's brand.

Your Personal Brand

Individuals can have brands, too. Think about the celebrities you follow. Some are known for wild behavior; others are seen as serious, or quiet, or "family" people. Each of these celebrities has a reputation, or personal brand. Some celebrities manage their personal brands very carefully, spending large sums of money on managers or public relations firms. Just as it can be easy to destroy a company's brand, it is not difficult to damage an individual's brand. You can probably name a few celebrities who had terrific reputations until a negative behavior was revealed in the press.

While you are probably not a celebrity, your personal brand matters, too. Every positive connection you make with a contact in your network adds to your personal brand. Also, every mistake you make in managing your image has the potential to damage your personal brand. As you work to sell yourself to employers, you also need to think of yourself as a product to be marketed.

TrueStory

"I have some employees who I call 'Excuse du Jour' because every day it's a new excuse. There's a reason why they're late. There's a reason why they didn't get the work done. Nothing's ever their fault. I give the better opportunities to the people who just get it done, no matter what's going on in their lives."

Professional characteristics (adjectives about the brand). What adjectives do you want employers to use about you? A common interview question is, "How would your best friend describe you?" When employers ask this, they want to know whether you have EDGE qualities. Are you Empowered? Are you Dependable? Are you Goal-Oriented? Are you Engaged? Think of a list of adjectives you would want your friends and employers to use about you, and do your best to live those adjectives everywhere—at school, at

work, and at home. If you practice behaving in a professional manner, those characteristics will become your brand.

Professional presentation (emotions about the brand). The emotions you want to create in your employers are confidence, loyalty, and trust. While employers try to be flexible, they really need their employees to perform the assigned work, on time and without emotional interference. You need to make them confident that they can trust you to do so. In Unit 7, we will discuss how to create a professional presentation that will elicit these emotions.

Professional values (values of the brand). Most employers are looking for employees who have a strong work ethic. They don't want employees who watch the clock and go running out the door the second their shift is over. They are looking for employees who will stay a few extra minutes if that is what is necessary to do a great job. They want people who are committed to the organization and its customers or clients. Think like an employer, and list the values you would seek in an employee. Displaying these values will be a powerful asset to your brand.

So how do you know what your brand should be? It's simple. What do people say about you when you leave a room? Think about that for a minute. Don't know? Ask someone. Promise the person full immunity and ask him or her to give you the good, the bad, and the ugly. A person with a great professional reputation is courteous, trustworthy, reliable, thorough, knowledgeable, and a team player. If you don't like what you hear, you have work to do.

Building Your Brand

Once you have decided what brand you want for yourself, you need to get to work. Building a career doesn't happen by accident. Those with successful careers—from neurosurgeons to pop singers—did not maintain their lengthy careers by accident. It takes a conscious act of will to succeed in one's chosen field.

You will need to improve your brand in three main areas:

1. **Education.** The knowledge and competencies you will learn in your Kaplan Higher Education program are an important part of building your brand. You are adding to your skills with current training, which will help you grow your brand.

2. **Industry knowledge.** This is different from education. In today's wired world, it's easier than ever to learn how an industry really works. It doesn't matter which industry. Whether you want to be a cabinet maker or a jet mechanic, you should learn everything you can about what's going on in your industry, including the big names, the most current developments, and the long-term prospects. It is time to network.

3. **Values.** Your personal values are an important part of your personal experience, but when we talk about building your brand, we are talking about your professional values. Employers will respect your commitment to realizing your own talent and to using old-fashioned hard work as a means of achieving this goal.

With these three big-picture elements in mind, keep actively working on building your EDGE:

Empowered. This is about fitting into the field you want to join. For example, men in banking and finance don't wear long hair and usually don't have facial hair. There's no rule against it; it's just the way things are. So think about your appearance and presentation. In your field, is it appropriate to have multiple piercings, visible tattoos, or an unusual hairstyle? It very well might be—but if it's not, then you should think about changing these things. You want to appear well-dressed, confident, and professional in a way that is appropriate for your chosen career.

Dependable. Show up on time, every time. Your employer is unlikely to congratulate you for being dependable, but if you are not dependable, you will destroy your brand very quickly. You can't be a good employee if you aren't there. Close doesn't count.

Goal-Oriented. You have an opportunity to surprise and delight your employer by listening carefully, learning what needs to be done, and then handling tasks without needing to be asked. If you can figure out what your employer needs in advance, you can build a very strong professional brand.

Engaged. Teamwork and collaboration are both critical to success in the modern, global workplace. Employers in small companies need employees who fit in well with all members of the team. Employers in large companies need employees who can work effectively across many teams. No matter what size the organization, you will need to demonstrate that you can work well with others.

As you think about your personal brand, focus on *authenticity*. Employers can spot a fake a mile away. If you're serious about your career, and you love what you're doing, it should show in everything you do. Branding yourself isn't about creating a phony persona to fool employers and the rest of the world. It's about being yourself, but in a tailored, deliberate way.

Traditional Networking

In Unit 2, we discussed networking as a means of acquiring job leads. Networking is also a terrific way to build your personal brand. **Networking** is loosely defined as the act of making beneficial contacts. In a career sense, this means meeting and getting to know people who have been in the field longer than you and who can potentially help you. When you enter any new career, it can sometimes seem like a closed club. It can be intimidating. You don't know who is who, and worse yet, you don't know how to get inside. How can you get started? By networking.

When you are networking to build your personal brand, here are a few reminders:

1. **Be respectful of other people's time.** When you meet someone new, keep your communications appropriate, brief, and on topic. If someone prefers communicating by email rather than by phone, honor that request. Be mindful of the value of other people's time. Time hogging is not just bad manners—it creates the impression that you're either selfish or oblivious.

2. **Be positive.** When you're talking to professionals in your field, remember that they have all been where you are. Everybody had to start somewhere, so complaining about how hard it is to get established will just seem like whining. Instead, let your natural enthusiasm show. People respond to enthusiasm.

3. **Ask questions.** It can be tough when you feel like the only person in a conversation who doesn't know the "ins and outs" of the

business. It doesn't matter if you're talking router bits or investment vehicles; everybody has to learn somehow. Ask questions and listen carefully to the answers. People generally like to answer questions—it feels good to be treated like an expert.

4. **Acknowledge acts of generosity and kindness.** When someone helps you, it's always appropriate to thank that person. This can be a simple thank-you email to someone for providing you with another contact, for example. For a more significant act, like recommending you for a job, a handwritten note is appropriate. However you do it, just remember to express your honest gratitude. Starting out can be hard, but remember: These are the people and companies you hope to work with for the rest of your career. And someday, newly minted professionals will approach you—and you'll remember how you started out.

Online Networking

Networking over the Internet is a relatively new art, but it is rapidly developing. It is generally not a good idea to "friend" your co-workers on your personal **social networking site** (on Facebook or MySpace®, for example),

unless you never put any personal information there. You never know where work relationships will go, and there could be enough personal information on your site to damage people's perception of you as professional. Additionally, what others post on Facebook is impossible for you to control, so control your professional persona by reserving your Facebook and MySpace pages for friends and family and by using a separate site, such as LinkedIn or your college's alumni website, for professional social networking. There are also many industry organizations that have blogs, social networks, and other ways of meeting people in your chosen career.

Here are some tools for building your professional social network:

1. **LinkedIn.** Once you have filled in your resume, you can use LinkedIn to gather recommendations and build your career network. Make it a goal to add a few connections each week. When you meet a new person through traditional networking, ask him or her to connect with you on LinkedIn. Soon, you will have many connections.

2. Blogs. You can create a free blog on any number of blog sites, such as Blogspot or WordPress. A **blog** is essentially an online newsletter, enabling you to share your thoughts on the industry, post photos, and perform other publishing activities. It is best to blog only if you have confidence in your writing skills and feel that you have new information to add on a regular basis.

3. Microblogs. Microblogs, such as Twitter, have become very popular in the past few years. As with blogs, it is best to microblog professionally only if you routinely attend industry events or have some other means of generating new ideas and content.

4. Websites. You can build your own website. If you are not a sophisticated designer, you can use prepackaged tools on large sites like Yahoo! or GoDaddy®. Building a website requires expertise, and site content can become stale if not updated frequently, so we recommend websites only for careers such as graphic design or photography in which portfolio presentation is critical to the job search.

Workplace **Tip**

Writing is a crucial skill for using the Internet. Proofread anything you post to make sure your grammar and punctuation are perfect. Treat the material you post online with the same care that you put into your resume and other professional correspondence.

Protecting Your Brand

To protect your brand, you need to think clearly about your image. Review Unit 1, Preparing for Your Job Search, especially the sections about removing compromising photos, asking friends to untag you from party photos, and triple-checking your privacy settings. To be safe, just take down your party photos. There are very few employers who want to see drunken pictures of their employees. Drinking may be legal, and you may be drinking on your own time, but posting compromising photos of yourself shows poor professional judgment. Even if you think you have your privacy settings set so that only people on your friends list can see your photos, it is easy to make a mistake in the settings. Better safe than sorry.

In order to protect your brand, you will need to control your emotions and monitor what you say and do. If you become angry with a co-worker, don't say something that could damage your brand. Instead, go into another room to blow off steam. It might feel good to yell, but the damage of one small outburst could last a long time. Remember, everyone's cell phone is now a recording device, and the Internet can be used as a free broadcasting service. Anything you say or do could be available for viewing by thousands of people within minutes.

As you manage your brand, you also need to pay attention to what others say about you. If

SCENARIO

You're just about to leave a nasty voicemail for a co-worker, and then you start to think better of it. What should you do?

QUICK FIX: Try the "YouTube™ test": Imagine that your voicemail showed up tomorrow on YouTube for everyone to hear, along with some funny images and commentary from its recipient. Would you be horrified? Would you be fired? Would you lose any friends? If the answer to any of the questions could be yes, don't send it.

you've ever seen one of those daytime TV court shows, you've probably come across a scenario like this: Person A sues Person B because Person B posted online something embarrassing, incriminating, or false about Person A.

It's unfortunate, but the Internet tends to lower people's inhibitions. People do and say unkind or inappropriate things to each other online that they would refrain from in person, and they have little regard for their long-term effects. Celebrities fall victim to this all the time—people constantly spread gossip about them and post videos and pictures showing them in a bad light. It can happen to you too, so from time to time, search your name and review what turns up. If you discover something unsavory, there are some things you can do about it.

First, however, try to avoid situations that conflict with your career goals. If you find yourself in a compromising situation or engaging in behavior that might threaten your job search or career progress, it's probably worth asking yourself a simple question: "Why am I doing this? What is to be gained from it? What do I stand to lose?"

Ultimately, you're the only person who can provide accurate and damaging information about yourself, through your own behavior. However, this doesn't mean that malicious people won't lie about you, doctor photographs, hack into your blogs and social networking sites, or even assume your identity. Whether done as a joke or not, this kind of behavior can be damaging, and you should take it seriously. If someone close to you is responsible for the prank, set him or her straight.

If you feel that you are being bullied or harassed online, contact the appropriate authorities. These might include police, school administrators, your boss, or even a civil lawyer who can file a small claims lawsuit. The important thing is that you stand up for yourself and protect your reputation, especially online.

> **True**Story
>
> "I manage a childcare center, and a mother called me up to say that she was pulling her toddler out of school because she found photos on MySpace of her son's teacher at a party, drunk out of her mind. I fired the teacher that day. Nobody wants to see their child's teacher in that condition."

Winning Through Branding

The modern successful employee treats himself or herself like a mini-corporation. Think of yourself in terms of your skills and strengths. What do you bring to a company?

What do you want to accomplish with your life? Your strengths are yours alone, and it only makes sense that you market yourself as the best possible employee.

Unit Summary

- Personal branding refers to the way you present and market yourself to others.

- Your professional track record, your style of speaking, your online persona, your appearance, your clothing, and your goals make up your brand.

- Networking can help you gain valuable contacts in your field.

- Social networking sites, blogs, and personal websites can be used to promote your brand.

- Use caution when posting material on the Internet. Don't post anything you wouldn't want a potential employer to see.

TO-DO List

✔ List three important characteristics you want to emphasize in your **brand.**

✔ List ten small adjustments you can make to your behavior, communication style, or presentation that will support the three characteristics that you selected above. Start making those adjustments today.

✔ Google yourself and see what comes up. Do the search results support the image you want to project?

✔ Identify five places—either online or in real life—where you can **network** in your chosen field.

✔ Set up a page on a **social networking site** (or overhaul your online presence if you already have a page).

Important Terms

How well do you know these terms? Look them up in the glossary if you need help remembering them.

blog   networking   social networking site

brand   perception

Online Resources

Tom Peters, "The Brand Called You"
www.fastcompany.com/magazine/10/brandyou.html

Dan Schawbel's Personal Branding Blog
www.personalbrandingblog.com

Exercises

Write your answers on a separate piece of paper.

1. Identify someone in your field whom you admire—it could be the CEO of a leading company in your industry, or it could be someone you know personally who is working in the field—and write a paragraph or two summarizing that person's brand. Next, list five specific elements of the person's work, work product, communication style, presentation, or appearance that directly support the brand image.

2. Write down five standard questions that you can ask people in case you get stuck for something to say when you are networking. Form a group with a few students, and practice asking your questions. Remember that your demeanor as you listen to the other person's response is just as important as asking the question smoothly.

3. What can you do to make your brand stand out over the competition? List three unique qualities you have, and write a paragraph or two about each one, describing how you will showcase this quality during your job search.

KAPLAN **success** STORY

Jessica Vendegnia
Westminster, Colorado

Attended: Kaplan College—Denver
Area of study: Medical Assistant graduate

My extern site was a dialysis center near the school. My first day on the job I was terrified! I made myself a promise to go in with a "can do" attitude, despite my lack of knowledge in dialysis. As it turned out, I found a greater passion for dialysis than I ever dreamed possible. Within three weeks, I was doing everything the other technicians at the clinic were doing. Because I was proactive in my own learning at the center, I was given more responsibilities and became a trusted member of the team. In my last week on externship, I was offered a full-time position at the center.

Professional Presentation

KEYS TO
success

Creating a polished, professional appearance

Adopting a professional attitude

Conquering your fear of failure

Choosing a corporate culture that meets your goals

Fine-tuning your image to fit your profession

Sometimes in life it is exciting to stand out, to get attention, to make a big impression. At other times it's important to blend in rather than to steal the show. At work, you want to be noticed, but for the right reasons. In the workplace, you are employed to be a part of an existing culture. The people in a given organization look and behave in ways that are appropriate to that organization. This doesn't mean you have to sacrifice who you are in order to belong. It just means that you need to present yourself professionally. You need to display the version of yourself that is the best fit for your workplace culture. Your appearance, actions, and attitudes all contribute to your professional presentation. This unit will help you identify and refine the ways in which you present yourself.

Look the Part

If you were an actor and you wanted to win a role as a rock star in a new movie, you wouldn't come to the audition dressed in a pin-striped suit and loafers. If you did come in a formal suit, you wouldn't get the role, because you wouldn't "look the part." No sensible director would hire you if you didn't look right for the part. It's exactly the same when you are looking for a job. Your professional presentation is the way you send signals to others about who you are as a professional. It is how you arrange your attire, grooming, posture, expressions, gestures, and actions to tell others what part you are prepared to play.

Dress for the Role

Dress for the job. This may seem terribly obvious, but it's where many people make mistakes in the job search process—right at the start. You have to look the part. In your personal life, you use your appearance to express your personality. In your professional life, however, your appearance should communicate your professionalism. All aspects of yourself—and especially your appearance—should be directed toward achieving your professional goals. Leave no doubt in people's minds that you mean business.

True Story

"Donald Trump talks about how he got started in real estate. He dressed the part. As soon as he graduated from business school, he went out and bought the best suit he could afford. He wanted to make sure he looked like someone who was successful in real estate, even though he was only just starting out. He said it was a little weird because he felt like a phony, but dressing the part is one way to make a great impression."

When crafting your professional attire, keep in mind the message you are trying to convey. You are trying to build the image of a credible, competent professional. Although your outfit may seem "cute" or "cool" to you, that does not make it professional. Err on the conservative side. Ensure that your clothes are modest, not flashy. Clothes should always be clean, pressed, and well cared for, never stained or torn, and they should fit properly.

Here are some common problems with professional attire:

- The XXXs: It is popular for women to wear shirts several sizes too small to baseball games and nightclubs and for men to wear cut-off sleeves and skin-tight tees. On weekdays, leave your tiny top in the closet and reach for a conservative shirt. Sexy doesn't always sell.

- The Lazy Neckline: Cleavage is distracting, and many people don't appreciate the show. Don't trust your own judgment of what's appropriate—ask one of your instructors what is appropriate in your chosen career.

- The Submarine: It is a popular casual look for young men to display their choice of underwear from beneath their jeans or to walk with a really wide step in order to hold up their pants without a belt. Just as women's cleavage isn't appreciated at work, your choice of undergarments is too much information and may be considered disgusting. You will need to get pants that fit and hold them up with a belt.

- The High Hem: Short skirts, especially miniskirts, are considered unprofessional in most work settings. (The exceptions are bars, nightclubs, and casinos, where they may be required attire.) Change your look so that people focus on your work, not your clothes.

- What's an Iron? Wrinkles make you look messy, so take those extra few minutes to steam or iron your clothes.

- Body Art: Some employers have a dress code prohibiting visible tattoos. If you aren't sure what is appropriate for the situation, conceal tattoos in order to look professional. If you intend to create and maintain a professional image, tattoos should be confined to parts of your body that you can cover. Tattoos on your face, neck, or hands may be unacceptable to employers in conservative industries.

- Pierce This: Visible and facial piercings may be prohibited in some fields for health reasons or by some employers' dress codes. If you aren't sure what is appropriate, remove facial ornaments in order to look professional.

- Put a Lid on It: Baseball caps and hats might show your flair or support for your favorite team, but they are best reserved for non-working hours. Many employers have specific dress codes that forbid hats or require specific headgear, and in some parts of the country, it is considered terribly rude to wear a hat indoors. Instead, keep your hair trim and neat so that you look professional.

- The Shoe-In: Appropriate footwear is crucial for many industries. Save the sassy heels, sandals, or flip-flops for the beach. Exposing your toes can put them at risk, even in an office environment. Sensible shoes of a dark color, low heels or flats, or industry-specified boots allow you to be more comfortable, mobile, protected, and professional.

If you have questions about the proper attire for your workplace, ask! In larger companies, you can talk to Human Resources. In smaller companies, ask your supervisor. Or, you can ask an instructor or staff member at your

Kaplan Higher Education campus, or try networking contacts or your mentor.

Clean Yourself Up

Grooming and personal hygiene are just as important to your professional image as your wardrobe. Appropriate hairstyles and hair lengths will vary from place to place, but conservative styles are the safest bet. No matter what the style, hair should always be neat and clean. This includes facial hair, and facial hair includes eyebrows, ear hair, and nose hair. The last thing you want people in a professional setting to remember about you is the hair in your nose.

TrueStory

"My friend's son got a job at a pizza parlor because he really liked the owner and thought he was 'cool.' He showed up to work on the first day with his boxers hanging out from his jeans, and the owner made him go to the store and buy new pants and a belt. Even when you're making pizza, you have to look professional."

Your hands should be clean, and fingernails should be kept neatly trimmed. Body odor might be acceptable in some cultures, but in American workplaces it raises a serious red flag. Clean clothes, regular bathing, and use of deodorant will help keep you fresh and odor-free. Avoid heavy colognes, perfumes, after-shaves, and body sprays. Some people are allergic to these products, and others find them irritating. Save the scents for your personal life.

ONTHE**JOB**

SCENARIO: One of the technicians you work with has been neglecting his personal hygiene, and clients have been noticing. This inattention to his self-presentation is detracting from your own professionalism. The situation has put you on edge, and this affects your ability to do your own job. The co-worker in question, meanwhile, is perfectly at ease and notices nothing wrong.

QUICK FIX: Talk to your boss. It is in your boss's interest to take action and demand that your co-worker clean up his act. If you have a strong relationship with the co-worker, you can address the issue directly yourself. Tell him that you think he could be doing more business if he made a couple of small changes. Tell him that you made similar changes yourself when you were working to improve your own professionalism, and ever since, you've been glad you did. If you can deliver the criticism with enough grace and good humor, he might even thank you for it.

Workplace **Tip**

If you smoke, do everything you can to avoid smelling like your cigarettes. Avoid smoking in your house or in your car, where the smoke will penetrate your clothes and hair. At home, seal your professional clothes in a closet far away from cigarette smoke. If you must smoke, have a breath mint afterward. Smokers often do not smell the smoke on their clothes, skin, hair, and breath, but others may notice the smell and find it distracting.

Especially if you work in close contact with people, pay particular attention to your breath. Brush your teeth regularly, and don't forget to floss. Because it removes food from between your teeth, flossing is as important to fresh breath as brushing is. Mouthwashes are a useful aid in maintaining fresh breath but are no substitute for flossing and brushing.

Workplace **Tip**

Having fresh breath is a good goal, but consider mints or breath-freshening strips as an alternative to chewing gum. If you must chew gum, avoid making sounds. Loud chewing, snapping, cracking, or bubble-blowing is distracting and unprofessional. Think about it: Does anyone look his or her best when chewing?

Act the Part

It's not enough to look and smell good. You also need to carry yourself well. These helpful tips will help you act the part.

Eye Contact

Like most social behaviors, eye contact means different things in different cultures. In the United States, eye contact is important to effective communication. Failure to make eye contact during a conversation can convey nervousness, boredom, or even arrogance—as if the person speaking is not worth listening to. Making eye contact during a conversation lets the other person know that you're paying attention.

When you are engaging in a conversation with someone, look at the person before you begin. When the person looks back, that is a signal that you have his or her attention and may begin. During the conversation it is natural to look away from the other person—constant eye contact can make a person uncomfortable—but glance back periodically to reestablish the connection.

Eye contact is also an important factor in taking turns during a conversation. When the other person wishes to speak, he or she will communicate this intention by making eye contact. Avoiding the person's gaze indicates that you don't want to be interrupted. If you look away until you are finished speaking, be sensitive to the fact that you are shutting down the other person's side of the conversation.

When speaking to a group of people, spread the eye contact around. Looking too long at one person signals to the others that you are not speaking to them. Try to move your eyes from person to person to let each group member feel included. This will help you hold the group's attention.

Expressions

It might seem like stating the obvious to say that your facial expressions tell others what you are thinking or feeling. Everyone knows that a smile typically means you're happy, a frown means you're sad, and a furrowed brow means you're concentrating. But few people have an accurate idea of how their facial expressions look to others. The only way to find out is to ask. Ask someone you trust to tell you how you look. Do you come off as approachable and friendly, or do you look apathetic or distant? When you are not talking, your face is communicating for you. What is it saying? Remember that how you look in a mirror—or in your driver's license photo—is not necessarily how others see you. Others see you thinking, talking, reacting, concentrating, or spacing out. Find someone who can honestly tell you how your expressions make you look.

Posture

Like your facial expressions, the way you sit, stand, and carry yourself communicates a message—a big one. If you walk into a room or onto a job site with your shoulders slumped, your head down, and your hands in your pockets, you will not look as if you are there to take charge and make a difference. You will look as if you lack confidence and are waiting to be told what to do.

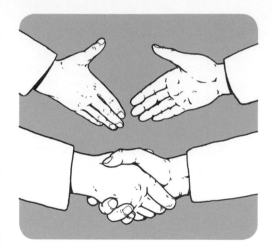

Figure 7.1 Demonstration of proper handshaking technique.

Exercise **Tip**

Exercise regularly. Exercise improves not only the appearance of your body but also your posture. To correct a problem posture, perform exercises that strengthen your abdominal muscles. Yoga is an excellent way to improve posture and make you more comfortable standing up straight.

Even if you are a slouch at home and are never happier than when spread across the sofa, in the workplace you must adopt the posture of a professional.

Here is a simple way to evaluate your everyday posture. Stand very straight in front of a mirror with your shoulders back and your head high; then relax and let your body take the position that feels natural to you. Did you just see yourself collapse a little? Does your normal posture make you look smaller? If you observe such a difference, remember this when you are in a professional setting. You want the way you hold yourself to increase, not reduce, your presence. Study your own bearing, and develop a workplace posture that is comfortable but that also makes you look confident, capable, and ready to take charge.

Handshake

Once you have improved your posture to where it needs to be, you will need a handshake to match. A weak, limp handshake is the equivalent of a slouching posture and a frightened face.

A professional's handshake should be firm but not overpowering. If you are a strong person with large hands, provide others the courtesy of not crushing their fingers. Clasp the person's hand firmly but gently, give it two quick shakes, and let go. Don't keep shaking someone's hand as you launch into a conversation. First, give the person back his or her hand.

Make sure your hands are clean and dry before you shake hands. If they are not, it's okay to say, "Sorry, I need to wash my hands, but it's great to see you!" Just keep the conversation moving: You don't want it to focus on your dirty hands. Never offer someone a visibly dirty hand to shake. You will leave them with a very unprofessional image of you.

Be wary, too, of extending a clammy, sweaty palm. Sweaty palms are unpleasant to shake and indicate nervousness. If you are on your way to a meeting and feeling nervous, dry your palm before it is time to start shaking hands. Carrying a handkerchief or a small pack of tissues is a good idea if this applies to you.

Cell Phone Etiquette

The pervasiveness of cell phones has made cell phone etiquette a staple of professional self-presentation. Although cell phones have made professional communication much easier, they also present opportunities for you to create a very unprofessional self image. Whenever you take a call in a professional setting, excuse yourself politely and hold the conversation in a private place at a low volume.

Cell phone etiquette boils down to a list of *don't*s:

Unprofessional conversations. Just because cell phones allow you to take calls anywhere doesn't mean you should do so. Holding personal conversations at work or school, in a public restroom, on the train or the bus, or at a restaurant or a reception can cause you to both offend those around you and embarrass yourself. Keep private conversations private. Broadcasting details of your (or someone else's) personal life, gossiping, or engaging in meaningless chatter all constitute unprofessional displays of both bad taste and poor judgment.

Unprofessional volume. Whether it's your ringtone or your voice, turn down the volume if you must receive calls in a professional setting. Use your phone's "vibrate" or "meeting" mode whenever you are at work, at school, or in public.

Unprofessional conduct. *Never* take a personal call during a meeting. Avoid taking personal calls at work in general. If you have to take a call while at work, keep the conversation very brief and go to a private area so you don't disturb your co-workers. Remember that employers are keenly aware that they are paying you for every minute on the job. Avoid wasting your client's or employer's money if you wish to be viewed as a professional.

Unprofessional texting. Never text while carrying on a conversation with another person. Your professionalism requires that you remain focused and considerate. Never text during team meetings unless multitasking is considered acceptable, and even then, keep it professional and brief.

Feel the Part

Have you ever heard someone say, "Fake it until you make it"? Every one of us has an external persona or "face" that we present to others. We usually do not show others everything that we think or feel. In fact, at work it is usually wise to keep your emotions under control and present a professional exterior.

Keep Your Cool

Keeping your emotions to yourself gives you a chance to evaluate each situation calmly and make decisions rationally. This is especially important for people who work in service professions in which split-second decisions can have serious consequences. Criminal justice employees must keep their emotions in check if they are to resolve conflicts effectively, trades people must handle their fears of heights or hazards in order to solve technical challenges, and health care workers know that remaining calm can make the difference between saving a life and failing to do so. Respected professionals present themselves with confidence, even when they are terrified. So, now is the best time to begin practicing your professional persona. If you have a tendency to become easily flustered, or even dramatic, try a new attitude. Begin practicing at home or with your friends. Try out some new behaviors. Respond to situations with calm confidence, as if you already were in your chosen career. If you act as if you are confident, others will begin to believe that you are.

Learn from Your Failures

Ask any very successful person to tell you the story of his or her success, and you will almost always hear a story of failures. Failures are opportunities to learn, to improve self-understanding, and to overcome fears—particularly the fear of failure. Only by failing do we learn that we can survive failure. Only by surviving failure, again and again, do we eliminate our fear of it and learn what failure has to teach us. Don't think of failure as something to fear. Think of failure as an opportunity to learn and of fear as something to conquer.

Build Your Self-Esteem

Not everyone naturally feels confident, so in addition to looking confident, you may need to practice *feeling* confident. "Faking it" is a good way to practice some new habits, but you will need to build real confidence in order to develop true professionalism. **Self-esteem** refers to how strongly a person values himself or herself. It is the level of respect that you have for yourself. Perhaps you were taught the importance of self-esteem when you were younger. Teachers and parents may have encouraged you to take up activities that build self-esteem. The positive feedback and personal satisfaction that comes from successfully meeting challenges—big or small—puts the focus on your strengths and increases your confidence, leading to greater self-esteem. When parents and teachers work to foster children's self-esteem, their goal is to make those children feel good about themselves. In addition, people who have healthy self-esteem are likely to be realistic about their strengths and weaknesses, willing to take on new challenges, and able to act independently. People who value themselves are also more likely to present themselves in a way that makes others value them.

Self-esteem is important to your role on a team for the same reasons. Individuals with higher self-esteem require less supervision, are more self-motivated, and are more likely to fulfill an employer's expectations. Remember, employers favor candidates who are empowered and engaged. They look for people who display confidence and work well on teams. If you lack self-esteem, a potential employer might wonder about your work ethic. He or she might have questions about your personality: Is this person dependable? Does she believe she is incapable of success? If she doesn't value herself, then why should I? Don't invite a prospective employer to ask these kinds of questions. Make self-esteem a priority, focus on it, and achieve it!

How can you practice feeling confident and develop self-esteem? Establishing goals and working hard to achieve them is a proven strategy for building self-esteem. At work, at school, or at home, offer to take on a new responsibility or learn a new skill, and approach the opportunity with enthusiasm and a positive attitude. Succeeding at new challenges builds confidence and gives you the courage to seek other opportunities to learn and grow. These strategies for building confidence are also great ways to build professional success. Few things will please an employer more than working hard to achieve the goals the employer has set for you. The best professionals are committed to achievement.

Set Yourself Up to Win

If you have a very rebellious personality and are covered with tattoos and piercings, it would be perverse for you to choose a career in the field of law, where professionals are expected to dress very conservatively and conform to strict behavioral standards. As you think about your professional presentation, it is important to think about the connection between your personality and your career and to set yourself up to win.

Think About Your Values

Your personal values are the beliefs and principles that you consider important. In the years following the high-profile corporate scandals of Enron, WorldCom, and other corporate giants, organizations have come under increased scrutiny for their values. One consequence has been that in some workplaces, greater weight is now assigned to the ethical principles that you bring with you into the organization. You should evaluate how well a company's values match your own personality and values. When your personal values reflect those of the organization, a good decision for you is a good decision for your organization.

Choose the Right Corporate Culture

Corporate culture is an organization's set of values, attitudes, and ways of doing things. In a way, it is the personality of the organization. An organization's culture typically reflects its founders' vision of what kind of organization it is, what it stands for, and what it believes in.

But corporate culture is also strongly affected by other factors, such as the industry the company is a part of; the company's age, size, and location; and how rapidly it is growing. Companies that are new and growing often reflect a culture of adaptation and versatility. Other companies might value stability over flexibility.

> ## Workplace **Tip**
> Learn as much as you can about the team you want to join so that you can assess how well your personality fits its culture.

Corporate culture indicates what a company values in its employees. Some companies reward individualism, while others emphasize teamwork. A company run by an adventurous entrepreneur might reward risk taking, while a family business that has been run for generations by the same investor group might promote stability. In a very large company, different cultures can operate simultaneously within different units of the organization. Not surprisingly, groups with different cultures will attract and seek out individuals with markedly different attitudes, values, and personalities.

Employers may look at your personality as an indicator of how you will fit into their corporate culture. Your personality makes a lasting impression on the people who work and study with you. More than any other part of yourself, your personality determines the image that people will form of you. Because personality plays a major role in how people relate to and work with each other, many employers look closely at personality when deciding whether or not to hire a job candidate. Some employers administer personality tests, such as the Myers-Briggs personality inventory, which categorizes a test taker into one of 16 personality types, based on answers to a questionnaire. Long after a hiring decision has been made, supervisors and managers look at personality when choosing employees for promotion. In many workplaces and organizations, personality is a decisive factor in employee advancement. After all, you are more than just a skill set.

Employers care about your personality because it is the strongest indicator of whether or not you are a good fit for the organization. Personality traits signal your compatibility with your co-workers and the type of role you are likely to enjoy.

Just as employers care about your personality, you should care about the personality of the industry and the culture of the company. If you choose the right corporate culture, you will increase your chances of a long-term, happy fit at your job. For example, if it is very important to you to have lots of tattoos and piercings, you should probably consider working in an industry or company culture that doesn't have a problem with body art. If you work in film editing or run a tattoo parlor, you will fit right in. However, if you decide to apply for a job at a conservative law firm, your chances of getting and keeping a job are very low. If you really want job security, you should look for a large, stable company. If you like a fast, exciting pace, then a small, entrepreneurial company will make you much happier than a giant "cube farm" corporate setting. When you are researching companies, look for clues to their corporate culture on their websites and in their materials. Set yourself up to win by choosing a culture that will fit you.

There are also some websites that allow you to look at reviews of companies provided by employees who work at those organizations. Glassdoor.com™ is one example where you can read about corporate culture, employees' happiness levels, and salary rates. Get as much information as you can so you can make an informed decision about the company before you accept a job.

Make Your Image Fit Your Career

It's all well and good to think about choosing the perfect corporate culture, but sometimes you just need to get a good job. If you're a hot commodity with a handful of job offers, then you can be picky about the corporate culture and the company's values. However, if you don't have these luxuries, then you're going to need to adjust yourself to the job. It's true: Professionalism does require a certain amount of conformity. But it's a good trade! When you build your EDGE, you will develop the tools to get and keep a job in your chosen career, so you can succeed, thrive, and build your own success story. Professionalism is the key to building the long-term career you desire.

Aundranique Fellows
Sun City, California

Attended: Kaplan College—Riverside
Area of study: Pharmacy Technician graduate

Appearance and attitude should be the top qualities you have when leaving school and moving into the work field. Your appearance says a lot. If you take care of yourself and look good, you're more likely to stay organized and also present your work in a good, clean manner. Attitude plays a big part because you're never alone in anything at work. The more positive you are, the quicker and better the outcome will be. It's also important to go the extra mile; it can sometimes make a big difference. Patients can tell when you care or don't care about them. You and your family members have all been patients or clients before; treat people how you would like to be treated.

Unit Summary

- If you look, act, sound, and otherwise carry yourself like a professional, you are well on your way to succeeding as one.

- Failure can be used as a learning experience.

- Knowing your workplace or school corporate culture helps you develop the best strategy for success.

- Choosing a profession that fits your personality starts you off on the right track.

TO-DO List

✔ Be alert for the next time you blame someone else (or society or fate) for a failure you have faced. Rethink the entire scenario and ask yourself, "Was there anything I could have done differently that could have altered this outcome?"

✔ If you don't know how, teach yourself to iron clothes, polish shoes, and sew on buttons. All of these skills are necessary to maintaining a professional appearance.

✔ Find something about your personality that clashes with the kind of professional presentation you want to achieve. Now work toward changing it. You can start by making a simple list of changes to implement.

✔ If you wear cologne or perfume, ask someone you trust if they think that it is too strong or that you wear too much.

✔ If you smoke, try to quit or cut back during business hours. If you can't, do your best to mask the odor.

Important Terms

How well do you know these terms? Look them up in the glossary if you need help remembering them.

corporate culture

self-esteem

Online Resources

The Eyes Have It: The Fundamentals of Eye Contact
jillbremmer.com/articles/communications/the-eyes-have-it

Cell Phone Etiquette: 10 Dos and Don'ts:
www.microsoft.com/business/en-us/resources/technology/communications/cell-phone-etiquette-10-dos-and-donts.aspx?fbid=pGjJZT1hg0r

Workplace Attire
www.helium.com/items/659516-the-importance-of-recognizing-acceptable
-workplace-attire

Company Reviews
www.glassdoor.com

Exercises

Write your answers on a separate piece of paper.

1. Write several paragraphs about a time when you failed at something important to you. Did you fear ahead of time that you might fail? Did you ever try again to do what you failed to do? How did the failure affect your self-esteem at the time? How does it affect your self-esteem now?

2. Write several paragraphs discussing the culture of your last workplace. How did the goals of the business affect the values, attitudes, and approaches to work that were encouraged among the team? What about your personality was a good fit with that culture? What aspects of your personality did not fit well with the culture?

3. Write a description of what you think it means to be an effective professional in your chosen field. What characteristics would well serve individuals working in this field? Initiative? Teamwork? Independence? Conformity? Creativity? What characteristics might be a disadvantage?

Interviews

Researching questions that are typically asked at interviews

Identifying your strengths and planning ways to express them during an interview

Developing answers to standard interview questions

Researching nonstandard interview questions and developing answers to those questions

Practicing your answers until you can deliver them smoothly and confidently

S
o the phone has finally rung. All that work—preparing yourself, tracking down leads, sending out applications and resumes, networking—has finally paid off, and you're on the phone with a potential employer. Suddenly, everything seems possible. You may feel as if you could have a new job in just a matter of days. And you should have some confidence: Out of all the resumes that crossed the hiring manager's desk, yours was one of the best. Time is too precious for companies to waste time calling job candidates casually, which means you've got a real shot at getting this job.

Up to this point, to the company you've been only a set of facts and qualifications on paper. Your resume and cover letter have done all your speaking for you. Now, by contrast, the company isn't just looking at your qualifications. It will be looking at and listening to *you* and trying to decide if you're a good match with the company's goals, direction, and philosophy.

Your task now switches to interview preparation and performance. Now it's up to you to personally demonstrate that you've got the EDGE (Empowered, Dependable, Goal-Oriented, Engaged). The better prepared you are, the more likely you are to make it over this final hurdle.

The Call

When an employer calls, your interview process has begun. Phone calls are common as the first step in the interview process because they allow companies to screen a large number of candidates fairly quickly. Many companies prefer to conduct quick phone calls before calling candidates in for physical interviews. Frequently, a human resources manager will make the call, not necessarily the hiring manager, so the caller may not understand the jargon of the industry. Employers often think of this first phone call as a screen, a check to make sure the candidate can speak clearly, articulate ideas coherently, and sound appealing over the phone.

Here are some important tips:

Be prepared. Think in advance about the questions an employer is likely to ask on a screening phone call. Write answers to those questions, and put a copy by your phone. That way, when the phone rings, you can pull out your answers and have them in front of you. They will help you overcome any nervous feelings during the call. Questions employers are likely to ask include the following: "Why do you think you would be a good fit for this position? What do you like about our specific company? What are your values? If we hired you, what would you do for us? How well can you fit on a team? How much money are you hoping to make?"

Find a quiet location. If you are not in a suitable location to take a call, let the call go to voicemail. Go to a quiet location where you will not be interrupted, and call the hiring manager back when you are settled. If the caller cannot hear you, it will not matter what you say.

Speak clearly. Professionals don't use casual language; they use formal language. They don't use curse words, and they avoid the use of "like" and "y'know." For example,

compare these two responses: (1) "I'm, like, into health care because I totally, like, want to help people 'cause it's totally dope, y'know?" as opposed to (2) "I want to work in health care because I like helping people." Whom would you hire? You don't need to use fancy language or put on airs. You just need to be clear and use only the words that are necessary to communicate. If you are used to very casual speech at home and with friends, you will need to practice. Create a study group at school to practice professional speech. This practice could win you the interview.

Be polite. In the busy, rushed world of our personal lives, we've all gotten used to texting, multitasking, and racing around. Old-fashioned politeness has been dropped for the sake of efficiency. In the professional world, politeness is not only appreciated, it is required. If you want to make it in your career, start conducting yourself with politeness. It's a requirement. *Pleases. Thank yous.* Listening. Following through on what you commit to doing. The things your parents taught you. Cultivate them now, and your career success will be your reward. On the call, listen to each question. Do not interrupt the caller. Make your answers brief and to the point. At the end of the call, thank the caller. It will make a difference.

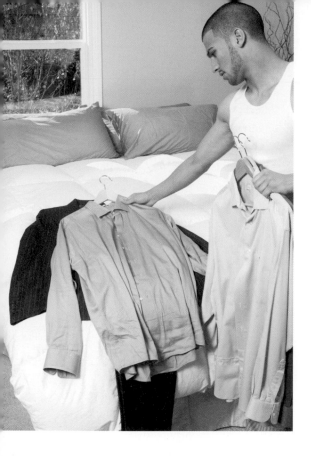

Have a positive attitude. Attitude is a little-known secret for landing a great job. When employers call you, they have already decided that you are competent to do the job. What they are trying to discover is whether they will enjoy working with you and whether you will fit on their organization's team. Many employers do the "airport test." They picture themselves stuck at an airport with you for four hours while waiting for a delayed flight. What would it be like? Do you have the right attitude? Are you negative or positive? Are you someone people want to be around? Attitude makes a huge difference. If the hiring manager can't picture enjoying a few hours at an airport with you, you're probably not going to get an offer. To prepare for this, start cultivating a positive attitude now—be positive about class, about homework, and about your future.

Preparing for Your Interview

If you get a call back to arrange an interview (or another call), you will know that the call went well and you passed the airport test. Congratulations! When you get to the interview step, your chances are about 1 in 10 of getting the job. These are great odds! (Remember, when you sent the resume, your chances were only about 1 in 300.) An interview is a terrific opportunity, so prepare carefully. You want to do everything you can to maximize your chances of getting an offer.

Some people don't prepare for interviews—they just have a fatalistic attitude and tell themselves that they could be asked anything, so there's no point in preparing. However, they are really wrong. Employers actually ask very predictable things in interviews, and it is possible to prepare well. A job interview is not a place to "wing it."

You should already have some good information. When you researched the company, before you sent the resume, you took some notes. Go back to those notes and review them. You should have a pretty good knowledge base. Even so, here are some steps you should take before the interview:

1. Do your research. Check the company's website and news reports to see if anything significant has happened since you sent in the application. If it's a public company, you can also check the stock price. Ideally, when you walk into the interview, you'll be current on what's happening at the company, including any major leadership changes, new product launches, and noteworthy business activities. Yahoo!® Finance is a free and easy place to find information about public companies.

ONTHEJOB

2. Prepare your answers. Just as you prepared answers for the screening phone call, you should prepare answers for the interview. Be sure to highlight the specific strengths that you bring to the company.

3. Practice, practice, practice. You'll definitely want to work on your interview presentation, from shaking hands to answering tough questions. Don't go in unprepared! Any kind of practice will help, but if you can get someone who has hired people before or someone who has worked in the field to do your mock interview, that is the best practice.

Types of Interviews

When most people think of job interviews, they think of the traditional individual or group interview. But those aren't the only kinds of job interviews. Your interview might take any of the following formats:

Individual interviews. Your first individual interview will usually be with someone from the company's human resources (HR) department. If that interview goes well, you will meet directly with a hiring manager or the supervisor to whom you will report.

Group or panel interview. There are two kinds of **group interviews.** In the first kind, you will meet with a representative group from the company. Common attendees from the company include human resource staffers, department supervisors, and employees from the department you applied to. In the second kind of group interview, job applicants are interviewed in a group to move the process along faster.

Dining or social interviews. In this kind of interview, you will meet with company representatives in an informal social setting, possibly at dinner or lunch. These kinds of interviews tend to last longer and have a less formal air than an individual or a group interview. Be on your guard, however—in an informal setting you may have a tendency to say more than you should.

Video interviews. Some companies conduct interviews by video teleconference. During a video interview, you might be asked to go to a local videoconferencing facility, where you'll interview with company representatives over teleconference. This interview style is convenient and less costly for employees who don't live nearby, but it presents a challenge because it lacks the personal factor.

Phone interviews. Even if you already had a screening phone call, you may have a phone interview, especially if you live a long distance from the company. Phone interviews have some advantages. During a phone interview, you can spread out your resume and your prepared answers in plain view to help prompt you. You can even have a computer on and open to the company's website. Also, you can easily and freely take notes during the interview.

Traditional Interviews versus Behavioral Interviews

Interview formats are not the same from company to company, so be prepared for whatever kind of interview the company prefers. In **traditional interviews,** job applicants have been asked questions such as, "What is your greatest strength?" or "Where do you see yourself in five years?" By answering these questions, the applicant reveals his or her background, goals, and ambitions.

A newer kind of interview is the **behavioral interview.** During a behavioral interview, the company is less concerned with your specific background and more concerned with your skills and actual job experience. Behavioral interviews are based on the idea that previous performance is more important than aspirations, so candidates are asked specific and detailed questions, such as, "How have you reacted to a major crisis at work?" or "Tell us how you handled an intra-office conflict."

Unless you know for certain what kind of interview you'll be facing, it's best to prepare yourself for any and all kinds of interviews. During your interview practice sessions, make sure you include both traditional and behavioral questions.

Staging Mock Interviews

One of the best things you can do to prepare is to set up mock interviews before you actually interview. During a real job interview, it's normal to be nervous and perhaps forget what you're planning to say. But if you've already practiced your greeting, handshake, and answers beforehand, it'll be much easier to remember once the pressure is on.

During a **mock interview,** it's important to act as if the real interview is actually taking place. Dress as you plan to for the real interview; take along your resume, notepad, and pen; and present yourself just as you plan to during the actual interview.

Job Search **Tip**

Go into an interview prepared with a 60-second story about yourself. It should include your experience, your skills, and your cultural fit with the company. It might also include a brief recollection of how you got interested in your field or how you heard about the company.

Choose an interview partner who is willing to take the task seriously. You can provide your interview partner with a list of possible questions and encourage him or her to also ask hard and unexpected questions. Ideally, your practice interview should be tougher than the real interview—there's no harm in being overprepared.

The most common questions asked at interviews—and the ones that you should be totally prepared for—are:

- What would you like to tell me about yourself?
- Why do you want to work here?

Your response to the first of these questions should take less than 60 seconds, and it should highlight your positive qualities. This response should never be about your dislikes, only what you do like and what you're enthusiastic about. For the second question, include at least one specific fact that you know about the company. Also include at least one specific fact about the kind of work you think you'll be doing.

Other typical interview questions might include:

1. Why did you leave your last job?
2. What did you like or dislike about your last job?
3. Why are you looking for a new job?
4. What major challenges have you faced at work, and how did you overcome them?
5. What was your relationship with your last supervisor like?
6. What was your relationship with your colleagues like?
7. What do you hope to get from your work experience here?
8. What are your long-term goals for your career?
9. Have you ever been fired? If so, why?
10. What are your greatest strengths and weaknesses?
11. Are you willing to work weekends and nights if the job demands it?
12. What is your view on the balance between work and family?
13. What do your friends say is your best quality? Your worst quality?
14. Are you a team player, or do you prefer to work alone?
15. What are your salary requirements?
16. How much did you make at your last job?

Your goal during mock interviews—and during the interview itself—is to handle any question thrown at you. Some interviewers like to try to throw off their interview subjects to see how they react to the unexpected or surprising. The best way to handle this is to have a list of your strengths in mind and find a way to slip one or two of them into your answer. Another important goal is to practice your personal presentation. Go back and re-read Unit 7 in this book as preparation for your interview. Every bit of the impression you make counts. Finally, in your mock interview, be sure to practice taking out your portfolio and using it to demonstrate your answers. Candidates can find it awkward to use the portfolio if they have not practiced using it beforehand. Be sure to practice using your portfolio. It is a powerful tool!

Interview Day

BE EARLY!!! For an interview, on time can actually be late, so be early. You need to arrive early enough to get settled, find the hiring manager, and fill out any required paperwork. Avoid being late at all costs. Some companies will even refuse to interview job candidates who show up late to their interview, thinking that if you can't be bothered to make the interview on time, why would you show up for work on time? It's best to arrive ten or fifteen minutes early. If you have to wait in the lobby or parking lot because you're a little bit too early, take the time to practice your answers and relax.

On interview day, it is important to remember that you are being judged as a potential candidate from the moment you are introduced to your interviewers—and even if interviewers aren't consciously aware of it, their perception of you as a future employee will be shaped by many nonverbal clues. You've heard these things before, but we are repeating them here because they are so important:

Clean up. Smell is a surprisingly important element in the way people relate to each other. Besides the obvious—being clean and showered—there are a few odors or habits that will reflect poorly on you. If you smoke, abstain before arriving at the interview if possible—most companies are smoke-free environments, and the smell of tobacco is strong and off-putting for some. Avoid heavy fragrances and meals loaded with garlic or other strong spices just before an interview. Do use breath-freshening mints *before* you enter the building for the interview. Never interview with anything in your mouth.

Dress conservatively. Interview attire should be professional and not call attention to itself. Although proper attire varies from industry to industry—interviewing for a job on a construction crew might not require a suit or a tie, but rather dress pants with a neatly tucked-in, long-sleeved dress shirt (don't forget the belt, and polish those shoes)—there are certain standards for business dress you should observe. And if you're not sure, err on the side of being overdressed. Things to avoid wearing to an interview include jeans, revealing clothing such as short skirts or skimpy tops, visible underwear or bra straps, your favorite "joke tie," flip-flops and sandals, and tight or low-cut pants or skirts that expose the midriff. The best option is often to choose a classic, dark-colored business suit. If you don't have one, this might be a good time to make the investment. You can wear it to all of your interviews.

Communicate clearly. If you need a few seconds to carefully consider your answer, go ahead and think it out before answering. There's nothing wrong with looking thoughtful and deliberate. However, poor communication skills are almost certain to cost you the job. You should avoid slang, swearing, mumbling, or talking too fast. Try to present yourself in clear, declarative sentences.

Project confidence. Look people in the eye during introductions and conversation. Shake hands firmly but not aggressively. Listen attentively. Answer questions in an even tone of voice. Smile easily. Sit upright and comfortably. Avoid slouching, leaning back, crossing your arms, laughing too loudly or uncomfortably, wiggling or fidgeting, interrupting your interviewer, or grimacing or frowning at questions you don't like.

Interview **Tip**

It'll be less stressful if you know where you're going before you head off for your interview. Make a practice run ahead of time so you know the exact location of the company where you're interviewing. Check out the area and think about things that could cause delays. Will there be a lot of traffic? Will it be easy to find parking? Plan accordingly.

Controlling Your Nerves

Job interviews can be nerve-wracking, even for experienced professionals. Employers expect some nerves, and it's not going to sink you if you flub a couple words or show a few signs of nervousness.

But serious nerves will not help you, either. In a sense, the job interview is a performance, and you're the star. Signs of nervousness include sweating, shaking, and stuttering. Nervous people are also less likely to pick up on subtle social cues and are more prone to making mistakes like laughing at inappropriate times or losing focus and not retaining the last few sentences that were said.

If you're worried about nerves, take a few steps to control them.

Memorize a few standard lines. This is where practice comes in handy. When people are nervous, they sometimes reach for words but come up blank, which only increases the nerves. Before the interview, memorize your answers to standard interview questions, especially if you think the questions will be asked early on. This will help you get through those first hard moments.

Practice your breathing. Deep breathing works. If you start getting nervous, take a few deep breaths. Breathe in through your nose and out through your mouth. Imagine your nervousness flowing out with each exhale.

Eat a good meal before the interview. Don't go in hungry.

Avoid too much caffeine. A morning cup of coffee might be a good thing, but don't load up on an unusual amount of caffeine. It will only aggravate your nerves.

Get a good night's sleep. The night before the interview, make sure you get a solid night's sleep so you're well rested at the interview.

At the Interview

When you are at the interview, just remember to be yourself. Keep a positive phrase going in your head—something like "I'm a great candidate, and they'd be lucky to have me," should do the trick. Just say it silently in your head over and over again. Thinking positive thoughts will pick up your mood and help convey a more positive impression to the potential employer. One good interview tactic is to remember to keep your answers brief. Just answer the employer's question and then pause or ask, "Would you like more detail?" If you're lucky, the employer will fill the space and talk a lot about the company, and the time will pass really quickly. If not, at least the employer will tell you exactly what he or she wants to hear, and you will keep your answers focused. Long answers can make you seem nervous.

Another important tactic is to use your portfolio. If the employer asks questions about your past accomplishments—such as, "Tell me about a time when you led a team"—you can go to the portfolio to show a picture of the team, the equipment you used, or the project you built. Visual images have a strong impact on the memory, and if you reinforce your answer with something from your portfolio, it will have greater power. You never want to just hand your portfolio over to the employer. Chances are very high that the employer will never open your portfolio, and even if he or she does open it, the portfolio will never have the same power as it will if you explain what is in it. You don't want to walk the employer through the entire portfolio—that can make an interviewer impatient. Just go straight to the section of the portfolio that demonstrates your answer.

Handling Tough Questions

It's a virtual guarantee: If you go on enough job interviews, a question will pop up that you've never heard before or that doesn't have an easy answer. You cannot think of every possible question, so do not be distressed if your interviewer throws you a curveball. There are some famous oddball questions, such as "What kind of animal do you most strongly identify with?" One candy company was famous for dropping a pile of candy of the table and asking the candidate how the candy was manufactured! The best thing to do if you get a really unusual question is just to go back to your prepared list of strengths and see if you can find a way to work them into your answer. If you can't, just keep your answer brief, and be sure to smile.

There may be some events in your past that are difficult to explain and do not reflect well on your status as an employee. Such events include firings, criminal convictions, harassment issues, or serious conflicts with previous co-workers. You have to be prepared to answer these kinds of questions. With modern background checking (see Unit 1, Preparing for the Job Search), employers can quickly and easily find out a tremendous amount of information about your past. Legal issues are typically a matter of public record and can be easily obtained.

Bankruptcies can be quickly discovered during simple credit checks, and problems with your previous employer can be sleuthed out during reference checks.

The first thing to know when you're dealing with tough questions is to always tell the truth. You have to assume that your potential employer is likely to find out the real story, and lying during the interview is a sure way to lose the job. If you are asked, assume that the employer already knows the answer.

Your best strategy is to tackle the issue head on. Tell the story, along with any repercussions or consequences that resulted. There are always two sides to every story, so make sure that you calmly and politely explain your perspective. But don't make excuses for yourself or become accusatory. This is the time for an explanation, not an excuse. Finally, don't dwell on the negative aspects of the experience. Just explain that you learned a valuable lesson. Let the interviewer see your integrity and your ability to learn. Instead of viewing the event as a negative that must be hidden, view it as an opportunity to show how much you've grown and how your current goals and ambitions have been shaped and tested by events in your past.

TrueStory

"I had a candidate I really liked, but the background check came back with a conviction for violation of a leash law. The candidate had checked "no" in the box on the application asking if there were any convictions. We really didn't care if the candidate had let his dog off its leash one time, but we couldn't hire him because he had lied on the application. By trying to hide it, he made it worse."

Remember, no one has lived a perfect life, and chances are, your prospective employer will relate to your past situation, at least on some level, and will respect your effort and courage in viewing challenges as opportunities for growth.

Another difficult question may be why you left your former employer. As we discussed in Unit 5, it is never wise to say anything negative

about a previous employer. If you do not provide references from your most recent employer, the hiring manager will probably not be surprised. Many employers do not provide references other than to confirm that you worked for the company. Even if you did have a negative experience, don't discuss it. Just focus on what you want going forward.

Asking Your Own Questions

With all this on your mind, it's easy to forget that your job interview is a two-way conversation. During the interview, the company may be measuring you to see if you are a good fit, but it's also your chance to get a good look at the company and see if you really want to work there. No matter how badly you need a job, taking a job out of desperation can only be a negative in the long run. Be sure to ask questions about the company's culture, so you can learn as much as you can.

Potential employers welcome questions during the interview process, and some employers may think less of you if you do not ask any questions. They may think that you are not really interested in the job or in their company. An applicant who has detailed knowledge of a company and asks perceptive questions about the company's culture, market, and goals is more likely to get the job than a candidate who seems incurious about the company.

Here are some of the questions you might consider asking:

1. What would be my various responsibilities?

2. To whom would I be reporting? Could that change?

3. What are the opportunities for growth in this position?

4. How would you describe the culture of the company?

5. Why is this job open? Where did the previous employee go?

6. What kind of management style does the company believe in?

7. Does the company prefer to advance from within?

TrueStory

"The candidate was qualified, she was confident, and I felt she could fit in, but then the ridiculous demands started. She said she had to make $80,000, that she had to have five weeks' vacation, that she needed to work from home at least three days a week, and that she had to have total control of her projects with no interference. She was off by about $40,000, three weeks, and a whole lot of cluelessness. I moved on to the next candidate without a second thought."

8. How long will it take for you to make a hiring decision?

9. What are the next steps in the company's decision-making process?

Once again, these are just a few of the possible questions you might consider asking. Be careful, however, in what you ask—even curiosity has its limits. During the interview, don't make any demands or try to bargain for immediate vacation time, schedule changes, telecommuting, or other privileges that are usually reserved for long-time employees. The only situation in which it's acceptable to bring these issues up is if they are "deal-breakers," such as being unable to work after 5 p.m. because you have to pick up your child from day care. Even then, be careful about creating a deal-breaker that will limit your chances. Would it be better to have no job or to find a creative day care solution? Be clear with yourself about what you *must* have from your job, as opposed to things that would be nice to have.

Questions That Cannot Be Asked

Although the purpose of a job interview is to match potential employees with employers, there are certain questions that cannot be asked of a prospective employee. Federal and state laws have identified a number of areas that are considered private and not connected to your qualifications to perform the job (see Table 8.1). These include questions about race, color, age, religion, marital status, citizenship, disabilities, and birthplace.

Employers who ask these questions are likely breaking antidiscrimination laws. If you are asked an inappropriate question, you can answer it, or you can try to avoid it. Be aware that if you refuse to answer the question, it might cost you the job—but intrusive personal questions are usually a symptom of an underlying mindset at the company and should be seen as a red flag.

If you believe that you were asked inappropriate personal questions during an interview, and you believe that you did not get the job as a result of those questions, you may have legal recourse. However, you should not accuse the company of anything without consulting a practicing attorney.

Table 8.1 Illegal vs. Legal Interview Questions

Topic	Illegal Questions	Legal Questions
Race	Any question asked to determine an applicant's race	Employer can ask about race only for statistical purposes and only after hiring.
Age	Any question about your age or date of birth, or any question with an answer that would indirectly indicate your age	If hired, employer can ask for proof of age (if hiring depends on being an adult or being less than retirement age).
Religion	Any direct question about religion, and any question about whether you can work on religious holidays	Employer can tell you what hours are required for the job and ask if you can meet them.
Marital status	Any question about marital status, number of children, pregnancy, or child care arrangements	Employer can tell you what hours are required for the job and ask if you can meet them.
Citizenship/birthplace/ancestry	Any question about your or your parents' birthplace or immigration status or what country you are a citizen of	You can be asked if you are a U.S. citizen or if you intend to become one.
Disabilities	Any question about disabilities *unless* the employer can prove that those questions are directly related to the performance of the job	

Unit Summary

- Preparation is the key to a successful job interview. Before the interview, research the market, the company, and new developments in the industry.

- Practice is also essential. Stage mock interviews in a variety of formats. Practice handling all sorts of questions, from both traditional and behavioral interview formats.

- Things that will send up red flags to your prospective employer include poor communication, unsuitable attire, poor interpersonal skills, and lateness.

- Don't lie about tough issues in your background. Instead, be up front about the issue if asked, and use the situation to show how you've grown.

- Ask questions about the company during the interview—you're interviewing them too.

- Don't ask about salary or make demands until a job offer is made. This is a very sensitive topic.

TO-DO List

✔ Compile a list of 25 questions that are typically asked during an interview. Answer all
of them, and rehearse giving your answers.

✔ List five things you feel will be weaknesses in
an interview, and list ways to overcome them.

✔ List five strengths you have that you will be
able to count on during an interview.

✔ Look through your closet and plan what
you'll wear to an interview. List any items
you'll need to buy.

✔ Set aside time for ironing, shoe polishing,
fingernail grooming, getting a haircut, and
other activities related to presenting a good
appearance.

Important Terms

**How well do you know these terms? Look them up in the glossary if you
need help remembering them.**

behavioral interview

mock interview

group interview

traditional interview

Online Resources

Salary Reports Based on Occupation and Region
www.salary.com

Strategies and Tips for Job Hunters
www.employmentdigest.net

Interview Strategies
www.interviewstrategies.com

Exercises

Write your answers on a separate piece of paper.

1. List the five skills or qualifications you have that you feel are the most important for success in your field. For each one, give an example of a time when you used that skill at work or at school. Give specific details about what you did and what the results were. Think about the best way you can work these examples into a job interview.

2. Pair up with a friend or another student to do mock interviews, taking turns being the interviewer and the interviewee. Use both traditional and behavioral interview questions, and practice personal presentation.

3. Write a sample thank-you letter after your mock interview, expressing interest in the company and thanking the company for the opportunity.

KAPLAN
success
STORY

Janet Clare Ricketts
Frederick, Maryland

Attended: Kaplan College—Hagerstown, Maryland
Area of study: Health Information Technology

If you take one thing away from this course, it should be this: Set goals for yourself on day one, be reliable, and always take responsibility for your actions.

The relaxed atmosphere of Kaplan College made the transition back to school easy after being out of school for a number of years. The teachers were flexible, and their open-door policy helped to alleviate some of the pressures and stress of going to college. Having teachers who actually worked in my chosen profession was definitely a big plus for me.

Follow-Up
and Negotiations

KEYS TO success

Remaining patient, calm, and careful

Following every interview with a thank-you note

Following up on interviews with professionalism and persistence

Thinking of rejection as getting you one step closer to victory

Negotiating professionally toward a win-win result

W hew. The interview is over, and you're leaving the office or job site. All that preparation paid off, and you presented yourself as a professional, with clear goals, strengths, and passion for your career. You answered the questions carefully and fully, and you feel you have a pretty good shot at landing this job. You know you've got the EDGE.

Congratulations! This is a big achievement.

But the process isn't quite finished yet. There were probably other job candidates who came in before you, and there may be more who come in after you. The last thing you want is to leave the office and immediately be forgotten. So it's important to follow up after a job interview.

The period after the interview is actually a hazardous time. As the candidate, you are likely to feel both relieved (that the interview is over) and anxious (for an answer or offer). This is a dangerous cocktail of emotions that can lead to rash actions. REMAIN CALM! The potential employer does not share your sense of urgency. In fact, this is the time when the potential employer is most likely to hesitate. Employers are making a big commitment when they hire, so they need to feel really *sure* before making the offer. You will need to be patient and careful during follow-up and negotiations.

Thank-You Notes

After the interview, it is considered professional to thank your interviewer. Immediately go home and write a thank-you note to each person for whom you have contact information. You should have the contact information of the hiring manager, who could be either the actual supervisor for the role or someone in human resources. You may also have received business cards from individuals you met during the interview process. Send a brief thank-you note to each person.

Written thank-you notes are distinctive, and many hiring managers still appreciate them. However, email thank-you notes are considered appropriate in most corporate settings today, especially if you were given an email address as the person's contact information. Here are some tips:

- Remember the advice about your email address from Unit 1: Your email address must be your name. If your email address is not your name, the hiring manager will not know who the email is from and may delete it as spam.

- Make the subject of your email "Thank You." Nothing else is necessary.
- In the message, thank the hiring manager for taking the time to speak with you. Be sure to mention that you would be very excited to work at the organization and join the team, and mention the one most important thing about you that would make you a good fit.
- If you can remember an unusual question or comment from the interview, you can mention it in the thank-you note, in order to help the hiring manager remember which candidate you are.
- If you have any information that might be helpful, such as a personal website or blog, you may direct the reader to it.
- Keep the note brief. The hiring manager is busy.
- Be sure to put your phone number at the end of the note.

Here is an example of a thank-you email:

From: jjones@hotmail.com
Sent: Thursday, February 17, 2011 10:30 AM
To: msmith@perkins.com
Subject: Thank You

Dear Ms. Smith:

Thank you for taking the time to speak with me today about the office manager role at Perkins, Inc. After speaking with you about the role, I am even more excited about the opportunity. I believe that my experience working at Jarvis in a similar role would get me off to a running start, and I am committed to helping you reach your goal of being the best Perkins office in the country by the end of the year.

I especially appreciated your story about how you built your career from office manager to executive. You are an inspiration to me as I start my career. I would very much look forward to joining the team and learning from you.

If I can answer any further questions, please do not hesitate to contact me on my mobile phone at 222-555-1212.

Sincerely,
Jennifer Jones

You should not expect a reply to your thank-you note or email. Hiring managers are busy and do not have time to reply to each message. If you do receive a reply, you should not draw any conclusion from that. Some organizations are more efficient about replying than others, so don't try to predict the future based on what one organization does. Just keep your emotions on an even keel. Remember, it takes about ten interviews to get a job, so some of the interviews aren't going to lead to job offers, and that's okay. Just remain calm and keep working on your job search—those are the keys to success.

Waiting to Hear

Many candidates blow a job opportunity with anxious behavior during the waiting period after the interview. You must remain patient during this time. Companies have many steps in their interview process, and they look at many candidates. Even if a lot of time has passed, that does not necessarily mean that you did not get the job. If you don't hear back from a company after your interview, it's appropriate to wait one week and then follow up. Candidates who reach the interview stage should be informed of the company's final decision, so feel free to check in with your contact at the

ON THE JOB

SCENARIO: After you walk out of the interview, you smack yourself in the forehead. You forgot to mention your volunteer work in the same industry! You know it would have been an important point in your favor. What now?

QUICK FIX: Don't worry! Go home and immediately write a thank-you note, mentioning in a sentence or two that you've volunteered in this industry and you're looking forward to working with this company, if they should give you the opportunity.

company once each week to find out the status. Do not call more often than that. Do not say anything impatient or rude to the hiring manager. Just keep politely asking the status and reminding the company that you are interested. Even if you do not win this job, the hiring manager will remember that you were professional and persistent, and you might be considered for another job in the future. Professionalism pays off in the long run!

The worst thing you can do during the waiting period is wait! One frequent mistake that job hunters make is to get excited about one interview and stop job

hunting. Then, if they don't get the job, they feel truly crushed, since they have put all of their emotional eggs in one basket. Instead, you need to keep your job search going. Keep hunting for leads, keep sending resumes and cover letters, keep setting up interviews, and keep doing follow-ups. One great model for your job search is called 4-4-4-4: Every day, try to find 4 new job leads, research 4 more companies, send 4 new resume/cover letter sets, and do 4 follow-ups (thank-you letters, follow-up calls, whatever you can do). If you keep doing 4-4-4-4, you will keep your job search going, even during the difficult waiting periods.

If You Don't Get the Job

Receiving a job offer is a wonderful moment, and unfortunately, its opposite—finding out you didn't get the job—can be devastating. Sometimes you will get a clear end point, when a recruiter lets you know that you were not chosen for the role. Don't expect detailed reasons why you didn't get the job. This is a sensitive area, with legal implications, and it's very unlikely that a hiring manager or company will give you a reason why you didn't get the job. You're likely to hear, "We've decided to go with another candidate," or "We're going to promote from within." The exception is salary issues. If your asking price is too high, you might hear, "We'd love to hire you, but we can't afford you, so we've gone with another candidate." Other times you will simply get no response.

Any kind of rejection is hard to handle. It stings. But it's important not to get angry or become accusatory with the employer. Your professionalism at this moment is very important. *Don't say or write anything unprofessional*. Just thank the recruiter for the opportunity and let him or her know that you would be receptive to any feedback that would help you with your job search. You might be in this field for a while—you never know when you'll run across the same company or hiring manager again or when another opportunity will open up at that same company. Don't burn a potentially valuable bridge just because your feelings are hurt.

Instead, take a moment to gather yourself, and then let the feelings wash through you.

Remember to approach your job search like a salesperson. Don't get discouraged—don't give up. Remember, the odds are that you're going to get about four to five rejections before you get your first job offer. Your job search isn't over just because one company said no. In fact, just getting an interview and making it all the way to the final stages of the process is a great sign. It's an accomplishment by itself, and it likely means that you will find another company that sees the same potential in you.

Use this event. People often learn more from their failures than their successes. Michael Jordan, one of the all-time greats in basketball, once remarked that he missed many more game-winning three-point shots than he ever put in. If you saw a highlight reel of him missing the crucial basket, it would look as if Jordan was an awful basketball player. But these aren't the events that defined his career. Jordan is remembered for the baskets he did make—and there were plenty. He used failure as fuel to become a better player.

A setback is just that: a setback. It's not "game over." So, let it sting, but then pick yourself up and get back on the job hunt. Later on, you'll be glad you did.

Discussions After the Interview

If you get a call back after the interview, it is a really good sign. This means that the employer is seriously considering you as one of the finalists for the role. Your chances may now be one in only two or three! You have come a long way. Obviously, your answers to the prospective employer's questions at this time are critical to your chances of winning the job.

Availability

Your availability may be very important. Employers often need help right away, so if you say you're going to need a couple of months before you can start in the new position, you could lose the opportunity. Employers expect to have to wait two weeks—because two weeks' notice is a standard courtesy for you to give your current employer—but if you're going to take longer than that, you should be prepared for disappointment. Most employers will not wait.

Hours

You will need to understand whether you are interviewing for a **non-exempt** (hourly) or **exempt** (salaried) position. If the position is hourly, then you will be paid by the hour, and you will be eligible for overtime pay under certain conditions. Hourly employees must clock in and clock out, and their hours are watched very carefully. Hourly employees are closely supervised. Salaried employees have greater decision-making authority and are expected to work until the assigned work is complete, so they may be expected to work much more than 40 hours per week. (Most salaried employees should expect to take some work home on nights and weekends if they expect to advance in their roles. Entry-level investment bankers often work 80 hours per week!) However, many salaried employees do not understand their employers' expectations and behave like hourly employees, running out the door at 5:30 p.m., as if a whistle had blown to signal the end of the day, whether or not their assigned work is complete. Employers really do not like this behavior in salaried employees, and during the interview process, they will do everything they can to determine whether you are a real professional, who will be committed to the company and to high-quality work and will do as many hours as are required to reach the company's goals, or whether you are a "clock puncher," who is just marking time at work to get a paycheck and will be a burden to them to monitor and manage.

During the interview, the prospective employer will probably ask some questions that are designed to check your work ethic. You may also get some questions after the interview. For example, the employer may call to explain the expectations about the number of hours worked and confirm with you that you understand the expectations and are willing to work those hours. Be sure that you really can commit to the employer's expectations before you agree to the hours. Agreeing is a good idea only if you are going to deliver.

Compensation

In Unit 5, we told you not to put a salary range on your application, but just enter "negotiable." In Unit 8, we told you not to give the employer a desired salary range over the phone, but to say that what is important to you is to find the right role and the right team. Isn't getting a job really about getting the money? Why all this tiptoeing around?

Obviously, compensation is a critical issue for both employers and employees. It is also a sensitive issue. Most companies go to great lengths to keep pay rates confidential—nothing will destroy morale in a company like people finding out that certain co-workers make more money or have a better benefits package. This is why you should discuss salary only when the employer brings it up, and only with the appropriate person. And it's never right to share wage information about other people in the company, even if you happen to have this information.

In fact, it's a good idea to avoid a salary discussion until an actual job offer is made. In many companies, the people conducting the interviews are not the ones who determine the salary. You might be interviewing with your future colleagues and supervisor. The job offer might come from a senior manager, a company owner, or even a human resources executive. They will include salary and benefits information as part of the job offer.

Benefits

Benefits offered by the employer are usually standard, applying to all employees, and you usually can't negotiate them. It is a good idea, though, to find out about retirement plans, health insurance, time-off policies, and other benefits. All these benefits are worth money, so you need to take them into account in any negotiations. A common mistake that entry-level employees make is to disregard benefits in the job search process. However, if you had to pay your own health insurance, it could cost tens of thousands of dollars—and in some cases, you couldn't get insured at all! Benefits such as health insurance are worth a great deal of money, and you should think of them as part of your compensation package.

Relocation

It is not typical for a company to offer relocation compensation to an entry-level employee. Relocation packages are typically reserved for internal employees who are asked to move to new locations or for executive-level hires. However, for difficult-to-hire roles, companies will offer some relocation benefits. If the company asks if you will relocate, you should

TrueStory

"I had an offer from the Andrews company, but the job I really wanted was at the Bellows company, which was dragging about making a decision. I called the owner of Bellows and said, 'I got an offer from Andrews, but I really want to work for you. I just loved your team.' Mr. Bellows puffed up with pride and said, 'Yeah, they're good, but they're not the same.' I got the offer the next day."

assume that if you say yes, you will have to pay the costs of moving. It is certainly all right to ask if the company provides relocation reimbursement.

Vacation Time

A very common error made by candidates is to ask for vacation time immediately prior to hire or within the first couple of months of hire. Most employers expect that you will take no vacation time within the first six months of your new role. This is so that you can learn about your role, get off to a good start, and make a commitment to the organization. If you ask for vacation time within the first six months, you can expect an exasperated response from the hiring manager, and some hiring managers will nix you from consideration immediately because they will consider this a sign that you do not take their needs or the company's needs seriously. A more common (and even worse) tactic is to spring this request on the hiring manager after having accepted the role: "Oh, and one more thing—I'm going to be in a friend's wedding in three weeks, and I'm going to need to take three vacation days, because it's in Hawaii. I'm sorry about that, but it's her only wedding, and I can't let her down." You may think that your employer will understand this, and you may get away with it, but in fact, you have just gotten yourself off on the worst possible foot with your new boss, who now feels blackmailed into giving you a perk that is against company policy. This will create the perception with your employer that you are unreasonable and unprofessional, and it may hurt your career in ways that you cannot anticipate. If you have an event coming up, wait until it is over before switching jobs, or give your best friend your regrets and explain that your career is important to you, but you will be able to arrive on the weekend.

Most organizations have standard vacation policies that include designated holidays and vacation time. Two weeks (ten days off) is a standard amount of vacation time for an entry-level position. If the position you are considering offers more than this, it is a very generous package. You should consider this as part of your compensation. Every paid day off is money in your pocket for time you are not working. That's a very significant benefit!

Enthusiasm

Don't be surprised if the hiring manager calls you back and asks something cryptic like, "So, what do you think?" You may not know what to say. What the prospective employer is asking is whether you like the team and the organization. Don't underestimate the importance of enthusiasm. Just as you really want to be liked, your prospective employer and the members of the team really want to be liked, too. So, don't be shy—tell them that you like them and really want to be part of the team. This could make the difference between your getting the job and someone else's getting the job.

Negotiating

You got an offer! Congratulations! This is the moment you have been working toward. You started with about a 1 in 300 chance, and now you have a 1 in 1 chance, or 100 percent. Now you will have a decision to make. It may feel a little bit like one of those high-stakes game shows. Should you take your winnings and go home, or should you go for something even bigger? Before you make any moves, you need to learn a little bit about negotiating.

Here are some important tips:

Do some salary research. In order to negotiate effectively, you need as much information as possible. Research how much similar positions typically pay in your area. You can perform this kind of research online (see the Online Resources section for a link to a salary wizard). Knowing typical salaries in your area will help you be realistic about how much you can make.

Remain calm. Salary negotiations can be tense, so keep your cool and don't make hasty decisions. Through your research, you'll have an idea what you're worth before the interview and what comparable jobs offer. Once a job offer is made, you no longer have to worry about whether you're a qualified candidate—they've already decided that you are. So, stay cool and take some time to consider the offer. You can say, "Thank you so much. I need a little time to think about it." Then, settle on a day to get back to them with your decision. One to two days is fair.

A week is asking for a lot, but they may wait a week if they really like you. When the day comes, call them right on time with your response. Don't make them track you down.

Remember that you are being tested. The offer and negotiation process is still part of the employer's test of whether you would be a good fit for the organization. Organizations want to know how you will react under pressure. If you become volatile or rude—if you crack under pressure—that may lose you the job at the last second. Remain respectful and professional, no matter what happens.

You may get the offer over the phone (a **verbal offer**). Employers like to give verbal offers, because it is difficult for a candidate to use a verbal offer to negotiate with a competitor. However, if you have a verbal offer, you do not really have proof that you have an offer. So, it is fine to ask for a **written offer.** You can say, "I'm so excited! I would like a couple of days to think about it, just to make sure I have considered everything. In the meantime, could you send me the offer in writing? Also, is there someone who can tell me about benefits?" This is a perfectly reasonable request, and the employer should send you a written offer.

Once you have a written offer, you have three negotiating options:

- Accept the offer
- Reject the offer
- Present a counteroffer

Accept the offer. If you accept the offer, congratulations! YOU HAVE A JOB! You have probably already discussed your availability and potential start date with the hiring manager, so you can just say yes and get busy transitioning to your new role. Saying yes is an easy and safe approach. Many candidates are afraid to just say yes, thinking that they are somehow "missing out" by not negotiating further. A common misconception is,

"Anything you're going to get, you need to get up front." Actually, you're in a much better negotiating position with an employer when he or she has seen your work and understands how terrific you are. If you try hardball negotiations up front and lose, then you'll never have a chance to show the employer that you are amazing. For entry-level roles, it is often the best strategy to just get in there and start building your experience and career. One important note: If you do accept the job, then you are committing to stay there at least six months. It is very unprofessional to accept an offer, and then turn around and leave after a few weeks because another offer developed that you weren't expecting to come through. Once you accept a job, you are committed and owe that employer a solid six months.

Reject the offer. Rejecting an offer outright is usually a good strategy only if you have another offer in hand. However, if you know for certain that you will not be happy at that organization or working on that team, then you should reject the offer, even if you do not yet have something else in hand. If you are unsure, ask the hiring manager if you can have a week to decide. Some organizations will move on to the next candidate; others may have time to let you think for a week.

Present a counteroffer. If you feel that the salary or benefits package is too low and you are willing to risk losing the offer, you may—after careful consideration—want to make a reasonable **counteroffer** (for example, asking for more money or better benefits), based on your qualifications and the job title. *Caution: If you make a counteroffer, the company has the option to walk away from the original offer and move on to another candidate. If the company does not like your counteroffer, you may not have the option of returning to the original offer, so do not bluff—only make a counteroffer if you are willing to risk losing the offer.* If you decide to negotiate, focus on the value you will bring to the company, not on what you need. Thank the hiring manager for making the offer. Restate your interest in the position, mentioning a few ways you look forward to contributing to the company's daily operations. Express your desire to be an asset to the company over the long term, not merely for a short time. Then present your counteroffer. Be sure to emphasize once again your interest in the company, and thank the hiring manager for making you an offer and for considering your counteroffer.

After you present your counteroffer, the employer has four options:

- Move on to another candidate
- Accept the counteroffer
- Reject the counteroffer and return to the original offer
- Present their own counteroffer

Move on to another candidate. If you make a counteroffer, you have effectively rejected the original offer, and the company can move on to another candidate. You may never discover that this has happened. You may never hear from the hiring manager

again. So, if you do not receive a response, you should assume that the company has moved on. A very organized and professional company will let you know that the company has moved on, especially if you follow up.

Accept the counteroffer. If your counteroffer is accepted, congratulations! Be proud of your negotiating skills and accept the position with enthusiasm.

Reject the counteroffer and return to the original offer. If your counteroffer is rejected, but the company says they still want you, then you must decide whether to accept the original offer or continue your search. If you really want the job and salary is not your primary consideration, then accept the offer and be thankful. Make sure you are grateful, not grudging, when you accept. You can say something like "I was hoping for more, but I am still very excited about the position and am grateful to be able to accept the offer." The same professionalism is required if you decide not to accept the offer: Make sure you decline politely. Thank the employer for the offer, express regret at being unable to accept, and mention that the decision was difficult to make.

Present their own counteroffer. If the company presents their own counteroffer, then you effectively have a new offer, and the negotiating process starts all over again. Negotiations can take several rounds, although this is unusual at the entry level.

Negotiations are exciting, and they are a sign that your job search is going well. Prepare to be flexible. Negotiating often involves compromise: The goal is to create a win-win situation in which both parties are happy with the outcome.

Crystal Kay Faxon
Omaha, Nebraska

Attended: Kaplan University—Lincoln
Area of study: Business Administration

If you take one thing away from this course, it should be this: Professionalism will come naturally when you have the confidence to become successful or be a member of a successful team. That confidence comes from education.

After high school, I knew exactly what I wanted to do in life. I wanted to work in the business field, and I wanted to be successful. The only problem that I had was not being confident in myself or my abilities. The teachers and advisors at Kaplan University made me feel like I was their only priority. They gave me positive feedback on papers and presentations, and by the time I graduated, I had a huge amount of confidence in myself and my ability to be successful.

Unit Summary

- After the interview, follow up with a brief thank-you note that expresses your interest in the job.

- Remain calm and patient during the waiting and negotiations after the interview.

- Rejection is part of the process. Don't be discouraged if you don't land the job. Bounce back just like a salesperson. Failures and missed opportunities are a part of life, so use the experience to become a better interviewer.

- In calls with employers after the interview, make sure to be enthusiastic and as flexible as possible.

- Research compensation in your field, so your expectations are realistic.

- Do not bluff in negotiations; if you are not willing to risk losing the offer, accept it.

TO-DO List

✔ Research salaries in your industry and geography. Be sure to consider your years of experience.

✔ Write down the things you are going to tell yourself when you get a rejection. Save them to look at later.

✔ Write down your **agreement zone**—the lowest salary you would be willing to consider and the one that would thrill you.

✔ Write down the benefits that would be important to you. Do you need medical insurance for your family?

Important Terms

How well do you know these terms? Look them up in the glossary if you need help remembering them.

exempt employee

non-exempt employee

verbal offer

written offer

counteroffer

Possible Agreement Zone

Online Resources

Salary Wizard
www.salary.com

Strategies and Tips for Job Hunters
www.employmentdigest.net

Interview Strategies
www.interviewstrategies.com

Exercises

Write your answers on a separate piece of paper.

1. Write a sample thank-you letter. What are the strengths that you will highlight about yourself?

2. Write sample answers to these questions: When are you available to start in your new role? What hours are you available to work? Are you willing to relocate? What compensation and benefits are you expecting? Will you need to take any time off in the first six months?

3. Pretend you are an employer, and write down what you are hoping for from a new hire. What do you think the employer cares about? What is the hiring manager hoping for?

Communication
and Teamwork

Observing nonverbal communication

Managing nonverbal cues that others notice

Practicing techniques for getting along with supervisors

Identifying the elements of a successful team

Avoiding behaviors that can cause team failure

Whew! You got the job! Congratulations! Your first day at work is a very exciting day. All that hard work searching for the job has paid off, and now you have arrived at your company or work site. Professionalism was the key to getting the job. Now, professionalism will be the key to keeping your job and advancing so that it becomes a rewarding career. In order to win the job, you needed to create the impression that you had the EDGE. Now, on the job, you will need to live the Four Pillars of Professionalism every day. In this unit, we will discuss the two *E*'s in depth: Empowered and Engaged. To be empowered and engaged, you need to master communication and teamwork.

You Are Always Communicating

Whether you know it or not, you constantly communicate. Communication is sometimes defined as the activity of transmitting information. It might be hard to see how you could go wrong with such a basic explanation, but this definition misses an important point about communication. It identifies communication as an activity, and an activity (like the related term *action*) implies doing something deliberately, actively. When you speak, give a presentation, send a text, or write an email, you actively communicate. Communication, however, also happens passively. You do things passively when you do them without intending to. For example, if during a class lecture you unconsciously lean forward in your chair and make eye contact with your instructor, you are sending the message that you are interested in the material being presented.

You passively communicate information about yourself often without even knowing it—by the way you look and behave. You passively communicate simply by sharing space with other people. The way you look, walk, and act sends information about yourself to others, just as the way other people look, walk, and act reveals information to you. Any time you are in the presence of another person, you are sending that person information about yourself—even if you aren't trying to communicate anything. It seems almost unfair, doesn't it? What if you don't want other people to know anything about you?

The truth is, it is impossible to keep from communicating *anything* about yourself, because it is impossible to passively communicate nothing. Simply put, you cannot control whether or not you communicate who you are to other people. Communication happens both actively and passively, verbally and nonverbally. The good news is that you have some control over *what* you communicate.

Verbal communication conveys information through speech or writing and includes conversations, phone calls, speeches, arguments, essays, emails, chats, and text messaging. If you want to communicate nothing verbally, you can stop speaking or writing.

Silence, however, continues the communication even after you have stopped speaking. Silence is, in fact, one of the most expressive forms of **nonverbal communication**—consider the "silent treatment." But silence is just one form of nonverbal communication. As you will see, there are many others.

Nonverbal Communication

Nonverbal communication includes aspects of how you look and behave: your gestures, your clothing, your posture, your facial expressions, and your body language. These facets of yourself always communicate information to anyone looking at you. And nonverbal behaviors speak volumes about who you are. Fortunately, by actively managing your nonverbal behaviors, you can help control what those behaviors communicate.

The Importance of Nonverbal Communication

You've probably heard the term "poker face," which refers to a facial expression that reveals nothing about a person's thoughts or emotions. Poker players are keenly aware of the importance of actively managing nonverbal communication. Poker players study their opponents' faces, gestures, and postures for clues about what those opponents are thinking. To keep from passively conveying information about their cards, some poker players wear sunglasses to hide their eyes and pull brimmed hats down low over their faces.

Effective poker playing means concealing—not revealing—information. Just as poker players do not want others to know what cards are in their hands, they do not want their opponents to guess the strategies they are pursuing. Successfully managing nonverbal communication can be the difference between winning and losing. Poker players take an active approach to managing their nonverbal behaviors. Winning at poker requires keeping an *active* grip on **passive communication.**

Understanding What Nonverbal Communication Says About You

Poker players have a word for a behavior that conveys information about an opponent's hand. A clue that a player passively communicates about his or her hand is called a "tell."

But poker players are not the only people who should be concerned with tells. All people have tells. Yours are those aspects of your self-presentation that *tell* others (give information) about you. If you walk into a building soaking wet when it is raining outside, your wet head tells people you forgot an umbrella. Show up to work at a commercial bank in shabby clothes and scuffed shoes, and your appearance tells customers that you lack professionalism (and that the bank's standards are slipping).

But tells go beyond your clothing and accessories. What if you stand so close to other people when you speak to them that they constantly edge away from you? What if, when you speak to other people, you never look them in the eye? All of these nonverbal behaviors tell others something about you. People who persistently stand too close to others when

speaking seem to lack an understanding of personal space, as well as an awareness of how their behavior affects others. Speakers who never look others in the eye make their listeners uneasy and come off as either lacking in confidence or, worse, untrustworthy. Bad table manners not only communicate that a person lacks polish, but also that the person lacks self-awareness and a proper consideration for others.

> ## Communication **Tip**
> It's important to be aware of your own tells and to understand what they communicate to others. It's equally important, however, to learn to read other people's tells. Get in the habit of watching other people and paying attention to their unconscious actions that communicate information beyond their spoken words.

Forming Opinions

You collect information about the people around you all the time. For example, if you were asked to think more about the person who sat next to you in your most recent meeting or class, you probably could recall if the person seemed attentive or distracted, fidgety or drowsy, prepared or disorganized. You might have observed this person for no more than an instant, but in that instant you passively absorbed a great deal of information about him or her. More important, whether you intended to or not, you transformed some of this information into an opinion of the person.

We form opinions when we decide what nonverbal communication *means*. Like the passive collection of information, opinion formation is not something you actively think about; it simply seems to be the way that you "see" the person. For instance, if the person seated next to you slouched low in his or her chair and stared at the desk while you sat up straight and followed the speaker's eyes, you might have formed the opinion that he or she was not paying attention. Of course, this might not be true. The person may have been concentrating intently on every word. The opinions you form sometimes tell you less about others than they do about yourself, but that does not make opinions any less important.

Most people unconsciously assume that a well-dressed person is successful and respectable. They also assume that a well-dressed person is more trustworthy than someone who is dirty or poorly dressed. Like your opinion about the attention level of the slouching person seated next to you, the opinion that a well-dressed person is trustworthy is at best a risky guess.

Practice
Critical Thinking

Think about someone who has recently made a strong impression on you, either positive or negative. Actively identify what led you to form your assessment. What aspects of the person's communication style influenced your opinion? How can you apply that knowledge to your own communication style?

However, people venture such guesses over and over, often without realizing they are doing so.

Think about it. Have you ever had a doctor, a teacher, a counselor, or a relative whom you admired, or around whom you simply felt comfortable or assured, for no particular reason? Now reflect on that person's passive and nonverbal communication. Can you find any subtle features of that person's appearance, manner, posture, or gestures that may have contributed to the strong positive feeling? Tells are not always bad. Passive communication and nonverbal behavior form a large part of what makes a person charismatic or comforting to be around.

Managing Nonverbal Communication

Managing your nonverbal communication is especially important in the professional world. In the workplace, just as at a poker table, passive information is often *actively* collected. People actively observe nonverbal behaviors when they want to learn about a person, as surely as they actively listen to and interpret his or her words. Further, people actively form opinions and make decisions based on this information.

TrueStory

"My business partner was 6'4" and 250 lbs. I knew he had a sweet personality, but not all of our employees knew that. One time, he chased a female employee down the hallway and yelled at her about a mistake. I had to tell him later that she was afraid for her life. 'Really? She's scared of *me*?' he said. He thought he was a gentle giant, but to her, he just looked like a huge guy."

Employers, job interviewers, managers, and co-workers all actively collect the information that you passively convey through the manner in which you behave and carry yourself. They absorb what you communicate, and they formulate judgments and conclusions about you. Based on your nonverbal, perhaps unintentional behaviors, people make decisions about your leadership potential, whether you look like a team player, and the kind of employee or colleague you might be: efficient, lazy, meticulous, careless, confident, untrustworthy, reliable, or a risky bet. When it comes to actively managing your passive communication, the stakes are high.

Fortunately, you can manage your nonverbal communication by becoming aware of the messages you are sending and changing those messages. An easy example is yawning. When you yawn, people may think you are bored, impolite, or simply exhausted from listening to them. You can cover your mouth or stifle the yawn in order to appear alert and interested.

In Unit 7, we provided a lot of advice for how to present yourself professionally.

> Most of this advice was targeted at making sure that you were communicating the right nonverbal messages to make a professional impression:

Attire. Wear clothes that are clean, pressed, not stained or torn, and modest, not flashy.

Grooming. Have clean hands, neat nails, and clean and flossed teeth; use deodorant, mouthwash, and no perfume.

Posture. Show calm confidence, stand tall, and don't slump.

Expressions. Keep eye contact, look approachable and friendly, and keep your emotions under control.

Gestures. Make your handshake firm but not hard.

ON THE JOB

SCENARIO: During your first employee review at the dental clinic, your supervisor tells you that you need to work on your communication style because patients have reported being unable to follow what you are saying. You are surprised because no patients have informed you of their inability to understand you. Your supervisor asks what ideas you have for improving your communication with patients.

QUICK FIX: Ensuring that your patients understand your communication means paying attention to their nonverbal behaviors. Make eye contact with your patients when speaking and study their faces and body language for signs of understanding. If you usually work while talking to the patient, stop working, sit down, and speak face to face with the patient. This will make the patient feel more comfortable about asking questions if he or she doesn't understand what you're saying. It also allows you to ask the patient directly if he or she needs to have any information repeated or further explained.

Actions. Turn your cell phones off, and listen attentively.

Now that you are on the job, you will need to continue to focus on keeping your nonverbal communication professional. You may not be the best judge of how you are doing, so find a couple of people you trust, and ask them to give you an honest appraisal, based on the list above. What do you still need to work on? You can't improve if you don't know, so ask.

Verbal Communication

Verbal communication is the act of using words to express your thoughts. When you speak, you mix verbal and nonverbal means of communicating. You communicate through the words you speak. But you also communicate through your tone of voice, through your posture, and through any gestures that accompany your words, whether you are aware of them or not. For instance, you might be speaking more loudly or sternly than you realize. If you are standing over a seated person while speaking, the person might be interpreting your passive communication as an emphatic statement of authority, particularly if you are literally talking down to them.

Listeners collect this passive information and add it to your actively communicated information. As long as you are aware of what information your behavior conveys, you can tailor your nonverbal behavior to accentuate the message you are communicating verbally. However, if you are unaware of what information your behavior conveys and exercise little control over it, your passive communication can seriously distort your message.

Own Your Meaning

Just as with the other forms of passive communication discussed in this unit, you can help control the information you convey passively through your speech by taking an active approach to managing your verbal and nonverbal behaviors. Through the active exercise of self-control, you can better "own" your meaning.

Here are some tips.

Speak at a reasonable volume. Particularly if you are discussing sensitive topics in locations where you can be overheard, speaking too loudly communicates that you are unaware of your surroundings. However, speaking too softly, especially when addressing a group, robs you of authority and makes it more difficult for people to listen to you. Avoid making people have to work to understand you.

Speak clearly. Enunciate when you speak. Move your lips and form the words. Mumbling conveys a lack of confidence and suggests that you attach little importance to what you have to say. Consciously enunciating also helps you accentuate your key points and clearly communicate the parts of your message that you wish to emphasize. Be sure that you know how to pronounce your words correctly. If you are uncertain of a word's correct pronunciation, do not use it. Likewise, avoid using needlessly "big" words. Speak simply and directly, or you risk communicating to your listener that you are pretentious, pedantic, or—if you use the wrong "big" word or mispronounce one—ignorant.

Be conscious of the speed at which you speak. Speaking too slowly can sound monotonous, and speaking too quickly can make you sound nervous. But at times either slow or fast speech may be appropriate. Fast speech can convey excitement, and slow speech can convey seriousness

or build anticipation. Try to maintain an awareness of the speed at which you speak, and vary your speed to suit your meaning.

Don't waste air time. Be brief. Never speak longer than you need to. Be wary of "talking to hear yourself speak." Respect other people's time, and do not waste it with needless words. The person who can say in a single sentence what for someone else requires a long, rambling speech is the superior communicator. When it comes to words, less is more.

Know what you want to say before opening your mouth. Decide what you will say, and then say it plainly. Do not be afraid of pausing to collect your thoughts. A pause is a wiser move than a hasty statement. Even though it may not feel that way to you, remaining silent while you decide what to say will make you appear much more composed than if you nervously fill the space between your words with *um* and *ah*. Pauses, in fact, can be very effective in maintaining your listener's attention. Skilled public speakers such as politicians, news anchors, and trial lawyers often write pauses directly into their speaking notes.

Be considerate. Be sensitive to others who may wish to speak, and listen to them attentively. Use gestures, eye contact, and nodding to convey that you are interested in what they have to say and that you comprehend their meaning.

Getting Along with Your Boss

Developing good communication skills is essential for getting along with co-workers. The most important relationship in your job is the one you have with your direct manager. Your boss is the person with the power to control your day-to-day life at work, and also the one with the most influence over your long-term prospects. Not all bosses are created equal, though. The following sections will discuss how to deal with different types of managers.

Good Bosses

If you're lucky, you will work for a boss who is in control of his or her responsibilities, sets clear standards, rewards good work, treats all employees fairly, and sets a good example. Some bosses are experts in the area in which their groups work; others are given authority based mainly on their management skills and experience. Either one can be effective; they just have different strengths. When you work for a good boss, communication will be easy and open—so take advantage of it. Talk regularly with your manager to find out how you're doing at your job, what you could be doing better, and what you could be learning. If you're interested in expanding your responsibilities or would like to be considered for promotion, let your boss know. If you do good work and show professionalism, he or she will protect you, back you up, and reward you as much as possible.

Bad Bosses

Some bosses mean well but just aren't up to the job of leading a team or managing personnel. A manager who is out of touch, flaky, unreliable, or misguided will make your job more difficult. That doesn't mean that you should quit, but you will have to negotiate a balance between doing your best work for the company and respecting the authority of someone who might not be making the best use of your skills or making the best decisions.

The most likely complication in such a situation is that your boss will dictate procedures that make your job harder than it needs to be. The first thing to recognize is that your boss is not trying to make your job harder; he or she has a reason for each request. It may just be difficult for you to understand the way priorities are set. In any event, you will need to do things the way your supervisor wants them done. If you do not, you can be fired for insubordination. In the workplace, you will need to adjust to the job; you cannot expect the job to adjust to you. So, if you have a tough boss, you will need to solve problems as best you can. Try consulting your mentors for advice.

Above all, avoid direct conflict, because nothing good will come of it. You can't make your boss into a better manager. But if you learn how to deal with his or her shortcomings, you might come to be seen as a valuable adviser.

"Ugly" Bosses

Of course, things can get worse. You may work for a manager who is abusive, insecure, or

ON THE JOB

SCENARIO: Your boss has just asked you to do something that you think makes no sense. What should you do?

QUICK FIX: When your boss does something that seems crazy, there are two possibilities. First, your boss could be irrational. However, the far more likely possibility is that there is something you don't know. Supervisors often cannot share all of the organization's information with all levels of employees. So, the best solution is to do as you are asked (as long as it is legal and does not put anyone at risk of harm) and watch and listen carefully to see if you can learn more about what is going on at the organization.

dishonest. In this case, every day at work is like stepping through a minefield as you try to avoid making yourself the target of your boss's wrath.

Depending on how "ugly" your boss is, you may want to simply assume a defensive crouch from nine to five and start looking for a better option. Sometimes the situation is toxic and not worth enduring.

> **If you don't have the option of shopping around, or if you have other reasons for sticking it out in your job, then you must do what you can to protect yourself:**

Document everything. Every time you accomplish something good on the job, write it down. Save every phone message and email you get from your boss. If there's no paper trail for some disputed issue, make one: send your boss an email to confirm that you're doing as he or she asked. If it reaches the point where you decide to bring a complaint up the ladder, or to human resources, you'll be expected to show solid evidence.

Don't provoke. Conflict may be inevitable with an "ugly" boss, but make sure that any dust-ups can't be blamed on you. Do as your manager asks, and don't start fights. Stay polite and professional. If higher-ups are watching, you want them to see that you are the one on the high ground.

Don't complain. If your manager genuinely is a problem for the employees or the organization, then it's fine to share information with human resources. Otherwise, do not discuss the situation at work. You can discuss it with your mentors or with trusted family members outside work.

Relationships with Co-workers

You probably spend more time during the week with your co-workers than you do with your family and friends. They're a big part of your life, and they can have an impact on your career—so it's important to use good sense when dealing with them. Always remain professional, and treat everyone with respect.

What Is a Team?

What's the first thing you think of when the word *team* comes up? A sports team, perhaps, with a strong coach, an on-the-field leader, and players who each have specific jobs? Or maybe a working team, with a manager and an easily defined objective? These are both good examples of teams, but they're just two forms that teams might take. Your study group is an informal team. Your youth group is a team. A good definition of *team* is "A group of individuals working together to accomplish a common objective."

Although a team is a group of people, not all groups are teams—and it's important to know the difference. Groups are not organized, and they are not designed to accomplish an objective. A group can be anything. All the people who go on a field trip make up a group of people, but unless the field trip is meant to accomplish something, the group is not a team.

It's no accident that our definition of *team* includes the word *individuals*. Modern coaches and corporate team leaders understand more than ever the value of prizing individuals within the team environment. Each member of the team brings different strengths to the table. A good team identifies each member's strength and uses it appropriately. If you were a football coach, you wouldn't ask your kicker to quarterback the team, right? And you wouldn't ask your quarterback to kick a field goal.

Successful Work Teams

While there are some workplace tasks that can be completed by individuals, most large projects are assigned to teams. For example, a construction worksite usually has a team of workers, each of whom has a different role, such as electrician, plumber, or roofer. In order for the job to be done well, the team must function well. Each individual must do his or her job capably and professionally. Now the EDGE skills become more important than ever, because your peers are counting on you. They expect you to be able to perform the skills of your role and to demonstrate the Four Pillars of Professionalism: Empowered, Dependable, Goal-Oriented, and Engaged. What if you were the surgical technician in the operating room and you forgot to prepare the scalpel or to bring in the gauze? The other doctors and nurses on the team would be very upset—not to mention the patient! Every member of the team has to do his or her part, or the task cannot be completed effectively.

ONTHE**JOB**

SCENARIO: You're a member of a small team that is introducing a new office procedure at your company. You find out that another member of your team is very much against the new procedure, because it will be less convenient for him. When you confront him about this issue, he says that if the new procedure is implemented, he'll quit. He's a good worker, and you don't want to see him leave, but you also want to do what's right as a team member.

QUICK FIX: Go higher up—to your team leader. You can voice your concerns anonymously, if necessary. Even if you're not sure about the negative impact of the new procedure, your team leader should know about your co-worker's concerns. And if your team leader doesn't know about this, there's not much chance that the team will do its job well.

They have a clear objective. Teams function best if they have a clear goal that is difficult but possible to achieve. Team members are inspired by a challenging project and by helping one another reach for the goal.

They have well-defined roles. It is important for each team member to understand his or her role and how it fits on the team. It is easiest for the team to function well when roles are differentiated.

They have predetermined methods for decision making. An effective team will have a clear decision-making process. This doesn't mean that one person will necessarily have total control over the team. In fact, effective decision making often occurs by collaboration between various team members.

They are diverse. Research has shown that teams are more effective when they are more diverse in all ways. This means that members of the team come from different backgrounds, have different skill sets, think in different ways, and have different personalities. When all team members are similar, the team can have trouble solving complex problems because the members' ideas are also similar. Diverse teams are better at solving tough problems.

They are supportive. Some of the best teams emerge from very competitive markets. This is because teams thrive in an "us versus them" climate. Teams bond well when they have a shared cause and clear adversaries.

They communicate directly. Effective teams can solve interpersonal problems because they communicate directly when conflict arises. Groups that avoid discussing problems do not function well as teams. It is better to be professional and clear in communication if you want your team to work well.

They share credit. If members of the team are focused on the project, not on the credit, they are more likely to succeed. If you want to help make your team more effective, focus on the goal. Trust that the credit will work out in the end.

When Teams Fail

In order to be seen as a professional, you need to do everything you can to help your team succeed. However, workplace teams often fail, and failure can reflect poorly on every member of the team, regardless of where blame lies. As you continually work on your professionalism skills, watch out for these common errors. You don't want to ruin your hard work and reputation, so avoid these *don't*s:

Don't gossip. Human beings like to talk about one another, and who do you really have to talk about besides the other people at work? It will be really tempting to **gossip** at work. However, look at the people who are really successful. They don't do it. In general, really successful people don't participate in nasty conversations about co-workers. It just isn't professional. If you find yourself closing office doors to talk or walking out of earshot or going away for lunch, watch out! Your boss wasn't born yesterday and will know what you are doing. People may assume that what you are saying about them

Workplace **Tip**

It's great to have a friend at work, but make sure you keep your behavior professional during work hours. Don't talk excessively about personal things at work, and don't spend all your time with just your friend. Make sure your friendship doesn't cause you to inadvertently exclude others in your office.

is worse than what you are actually saying. Just don't do it. Gossip is unprofessional. Instead, talk about your favorite sports team or soap star or TV show—keep it fun and light.

Don't let friendships get in the way of work. Many people make lifelong friends in the workplace. That's great, but remember that your primary purpose there is to do your job and advance your career, not to make friends. Set your sights on being part of a good team. If you end up making friends along the way, fine; just keep your priorities straight. Remember that once you're friends with someone, you owe each other a loyalty that can come into conflict with your duties at work. What do you do if your friend is doing a lousy job and dragging down the whole team? What if your friend

> ### Practice Critical Thinking
>
> How can you use a company social function as an opportunity to make connections and advance your career? Should you dance? Participate in karaoke? Well, there are some things that a book just can't tell you. Use your best judgment.

comes into conflict with the boss—or with another friend at work? Be aware of these things as you're getting to know people, and choose your friends wisely.

Don't date co-workers. If you get romantically involved with a co-worker, be prepared to deal with some thorny issues. For starters, many organizations have policies about employee dating. Some will require you to disclose your relationship, or even declare that you can't both work in the same department. You may consider your love life to be none of the company's business, but private companies in most states can make it their business—they can even discipline or fire you for not following their policies. Don't think that you can keep the relationship a secret; chances are high that you can't. Even if it doesn't put your job at risk, dating a co-worker is unprofessional. You can't be objective about your boyfriend's or girlfriend's work, and your loyalties will be confused at best. Both your judgment and that of the employee you are dating will be seen as biased—and rightly so. And, worst of all, breaking up with a co-worker can be terrible. You'll still have to see each other every day, you may have to work closely together on a project, and everyone will be watching and talking about you both.

Don't conduct personal business at work. If you spend the entire business day at work, it makes it tricky to handle calls to your doctor, the bank, your realtor, the plumber, or your kids' school, or to deal with any of the other complications of life that can intrude on your workday. Most employers and co-workers understand that

sometimes you have to deal with **personal business** while at work, but they expect you to keep it to a minimum. If any obligation can be handled before or after work or on your lunch hour, do it then. If you must take a call at your desk or access your personal email account, make it as quick as possible. It might be better to take your cell phone outside or to the break room rather than disrupt your co-workers by talking about personal business.

Don't get drunk at the company party. There is no better way to ruin your professional reputation and damage your team dynamics than to do something out of bounds during off-work hours. Company social functions offer you and your co-workers a chance to see sides of each other that you never see during the workday, and to get to like each other better. Got that? You want to be liked *better*. So don't treat a company function as a house party. If alcohol is served, feel free to enjoy a drink—not three or four. Loosen up a little, yes, but don't say anything you wouldn't want to hear repeated Monday

Workplace **Tip**

Set your cell phone on vibrate, and keep it with you. That way, you won't have to worry about your cell phone ringing endlessly when you're away from your work area. No one likes to listen to the ringtone of an absent co-worker's unanswered cell phone.

morning. Avoid any overindulgence, off-color jokes, foul language, and crude or sexual comments.

Don't do anything you wouldn't want to tell your parents about. If you lie, or cheat, or violate company policy, or fail to practice **business etiquette**, one of your co-workers will notice. Poor behavior on your part can break down the team, as co-workers will need to decide whether to turn you in, join you, or stew in silence. Know the company's policies about breaks, sick days, visitors, music, personal use of company resources, and other areas that could cause conflict with your co-workers. By being a solid team member, you'll do your part to create an upbeat work environment.

KAPLAN
success
STORY

Stephanie Jean Bivens
Hagerstown, Maryland

Attended: Kaplan University—Hagerstown
Area of study: Business Administration—Emphasis in Accounting
Position/Employer: Bookkeeper/Bookstore Manager, Kaplan University—Hagerstown

If you take one thing away from this course, it should be this: Always remember that you are a part of a team effort, and in order for this effort to work, you have to be positive no matter what the job at hand is.

Kaplan has helped me by giving me the opportunity to work with them. I have always known education is very important, but working with Kaplan has taught me how to reach this out to others. No matter what happens with your job, no one can take your education away, and Kaplan has been able to teach this to many.

Unit Summary

- Understanding the full range of ways in which you communicate will make you a more effective communicator.

- Nonverbal behavior, even when it communicates passively, is often observed actively in the workplace.

- Understanding and practicing your communication behaviors will help ensure that your meaning is communicated intact, which reduces the risks posed by misunderstanding and misinterpretation.

- If you work for an attentive, responsible, effective manager, you have the opportunity to enhance your career prospects by communicating regularly about your job performance and professional goals.

- When working for an abusive manager, document everything and don't look for trouble.

- Teams are groups of individuals, all working toward the same goal or objective.

- Teams use strengths from all their members. Good teams are diverse in terms of their members' strengths.

TO-DO List

- ✔ Record the nonverbal behaviors that you observe in people you see every day. What do these cues tell you about each person?

- ✔ Observe the way service professionals, such as waiters and cashiers, respond to you. What do you think your appearance, behavior, and comportment tell them about you?

- ✔ Identify one of your tells that you would like to get rid of. How will you go about doing so?

- ✔ List the three most important qualities in a co-worker, and resolve to demonstrate those in your workplace behavior.

- ✔ Come up with several topics that are appropriate for workplace conversation.

- ✔ List five qualities of a successful team, and explain each.

Important Terms

How well do you know these terms? Look them up in the glossary if you need help remembering them.

verbal communication	**nonverbal communication**
business etiquette	**passive communication**
gossip	**personal business**

Online Resources

**Communicating and Building Relationships
(free PDF download) at Dale Carnegie**
www.dalecarnegie.com

Communication Skills Self-Assessment
http://spot.pcc.edu/~rjacobs/career/effective_communication_skills.htm

How to Get Along with Your Co-workers
http://hubpages.com/hub/how-to-get-along-with-your-coworkers

Exercises

Write your answers on a separate piece of paper.

1. Write as accurate an assessment as you can of your own passive communication behaviors. What do you do around others that might communicate more information about yourself than you wish to share? (What are your tells?) What nonverbal behaviors might communicate positive aspects of yourself (e.g., that you are a good listener, are patient, or are understanding)?

2. Write down three company behavioral rules that you would like an employer to enforce. Remember, these rules are in place to protect employees and their ability to succeed at work, not just to restrict what employees can do on the job.

3. Write a short essay (one to two pages) describing a successful team that you admire. Remember that the term *team* can be broadly applied. The team you choose could be a corporation or a sports team, or it could be a more informal group. The important thing to focus on is that a team is made up of many individuals working toward a common goal. In your paper, identify the various strengths of the individual team members and write about how each team member contributes to the success of the team.

UNIT
11

Managing
Finances

Creating a monthly budget to ensure that all of your expenses are paid on time

Developing responsible habits for using credit and managing debt

Adopting sensible safety practices to protect yourself from identity theft and related crimes

Investing cautiously and wisely to build on your financial assets

Taking full advantage of employee benefits such as medical insurance and retirement plans

m ost purchases have only short-term value. When you buy food, you usually intend to eat it within a short period of time. After you eat it, it has no further value. When you buy electronics, like a TV or stereo or phone, they will last a little longer; they cost more because their value lasts longer. There are some purchases, however, that not only have long-term value, but also are considered an investment—that is, as a result of the purchase, you may make more money later. The two most expensive investments that most people make in their lives are the purchase of a home and the costs associated with obtaining higher education (Collis, 1999).[1] In both cases, the purchasers spend with the intention that the investments will pay off. (The home buyer hopes the price of the house will rise, and the college graduate hopes that his or her salary potential will increase.) But these investments are so large that they require planning. You will need to pay your mortgage and your student loans in installments, over a long period of time. In order to make the most from your investments and come out ahead, you will need to plan carefully. In this unit, we will discuss how you can manage your spending to keep your finances in order.

[1] Collis, D. J. (1999). When industries change: Scenarios for higher education. In *Forum Futures: 2000 Papers*, Vol. 3. Retrieved from www-cdn.educause.edu

Basic Money Management

Once you move from lower-level jobs into a career, you're likely to see a sizable hike in your paycheck. Not surprisingly, there are many more things that you will have to spend money on as a professional—appropriate clothes, regular transportation, meals and coffee on the go, and perhaps child care or mortgage payments.

Many people think they can get by just by winging it: Find a bill in the mail, and pay it if there's enough money to do so; if not, wait; and repeat as necessary. It turns out that when you didn't pay the cable bill, the company helpfully tacked it onto the next month's bill. If the company cut your service, you paid them off and let the phone bill slide, or put all your groceries on a credit card for a while. After years of letting things "work themselves out," you have experienced some lean times, paid some overdraft fees, and received some collection calls; but you've never gone to jail or anything, so everything's fine—right?

Wrong. You may be able to play the system in the short term. By doing so, however, you only create much bigger problems for yourself in the long term. If you don't develop a system for managing your money and expenses, you could end up paying thousands of dollars in unnecessary interest; you could lose your car or your home; and you definitely will damage your credit score, which can put any car, any home, and perhaps even certain jobs out of your reach.

Creating Your Budget

There is no way around it: You have to draw up a **budget.** Many software packages, such as Quicken®, provide a ready-made template and do all the math for you. A spreadsheet program such as Microsoft® Excel® also does the trick cheaply and easily. But one way or another, you need to track and plan for your income and expenses.

A basic budget table will keep track of how much money comes in, how much goes out, and when it moves. Figure 11.1 shows a typical monthly budget table. To keep track of your monthly expenses, document the following items:

- **Date:** When a bill is due and when it is paid.
- **Item:** The name of an expense (for example, *Gas bill*).
- **Budgeted amount:** The amount you plan to spend for the item. Income is positive ($1,100) and expenses are negative (–$420). You need to enter this information ahead of time.
- **Actual amount:** The amount you actually spent or received for an item budgeted earlier. Comparing the budgeted and actual amounts can help you identify places where your budgeting is off.
- **Balance:** The amount of money left in your bank account after you adjust for each item.

Most bills come on a monthly basis, so plan to budget month by month.

Calculating Expenses

The key to successful budgeting is knowing as much as possible ahead of time. If your income is predictable, you don't have to spend much time thinking about that. Just make sure you budget for your *net* pay—the amount of your check—and not your *gross* pay, before taxes and other deductions are taken out. If you're paid on commission or if your work hours vary from week to week, make your best estimate.

Many expenses will also be fixed: Your cable bill is probably the same every month, as are your cell phone bill, your rent or mortgage payment, your student loan payment, your car insurance, and so on. You should try to make the same true for as many of your

Income Source:

Net Income Total Amount:

		Amount	Date Due	Date Paid
Fixed Amounts	Mortgage/Rent			
	Car Payment			
	Tuition Payment			
	Student Loan Payment			
	Other Loans			
	Internet Access			
	Day Care			
	Insurance			
	Clubs/Dues			
	Savings			
	Allowance/Mad Money			
Fixed Variable	Electricity			
	Oil/Gas			
	Water/Garbage			
	Telephone/Cell Phone			
	Cable TV/Satellite			
	Groceries			
	Meals Out			
	Auto Expense/Gas			
	Church/Charity			
Occasional	Household			
	Personal			
	Clothes			
	Medical			
	Child Expenses			
	Recreation			
Installment	Credit Cards			
Total	Total Income			
	Total Expenses			
	Total Excess			
	Total Short			

Figure 11.1 Monthly budget table

bills as possible. For instance, your power company may offer a budget plan in which each month you make a fixed payment based on an estimated average of your heating bills for the whole year. That way, you pay a little extra during the summer, but you don't have huge bills in the winter.

Expenses that can't be fixed must be controlled. Set out a specific amount each week for groceries. Save all grocery receipts for a month to see how much you spend on average. Do the same for everything else you spend money on: filling your gas tank, eating out, going to the movies, and so on. If you don't want to budget every single small expense, then consider budgeting a certain amount each week for petty cash. Each Sunday, take out your "allowance" from an ATM, and use that cash to pay for all the week's little expenses. Don't break out your debit card, and don't take out any more cash until the next week.

Some expenses don't come up every month. For instance, you might pay $40 four times a year for an oil change, or you might take the dog to the vet for a checkup every six months. Any long-term expense that you know is coming should be planned for. Set aside a certain amount each month so that when it comes time to pay, you can do it without raiding your bank account.

Practice Critical Thinking

Step 1: Look at what you spend now.

Step 2: Ask yourself what you really *need* to spend. What area of your spending could be better handled? Many people find that they can save a lot of money just by changing a habit. They might quit buying $4-a-cup coffee and start making their own coffee instead.

Spending Diary

Directions : Record everything that you spend each day in the categories provided. You can indicate the use of a credit card with (CR). Remember that if you do not pay off the credit card balance for the month you will have to pay interest on your purchases. Make additional copies as needed.

Week of: _____

Day	Total Spending	Housing/ Utilities	Bills/ Education	Food	Transportation/ Auto	Health	Personal/ Entertainment	Other Expenses
Example	$108	$55 (utilities bill)	$1 (notebook)	$30 (all meals)	$20 (gas) (CR)		$2 (DVD Rental)	
Sunday								
Monday								
Tuesday								
Wednesday								
Thursday								
Friday								
Saturday								

Remember: You are trying to find out where your "money leakage" is occurring. Those small expenses do add up over time!
Example: The average fast food combo meal (the combo + tax) twice per week for a year would cost about **$587 per year.**

Figure 11.2 Spending diary

Also, as contradictory as it may sound, plan for surprises: Open a savings account, and budget at least a small amount from each paycheck to deposit there; most banks will let you set up an automatic transfer. Even $20 a month will add up over time. Set a goal to build up an "emergency fund" that could cover three months' worth of living expenses. A savings account pays a small amount of interest on your deposits, but its real value lies in keeping a block of money separate from your regular spending.

Staying on Budget

Once you've accounted for all your expenses, it's time to take control of them. You may find that your monthly expenses total more than your monthly income. In that case, review your expenses and see what you can cut. Maybe you can scale back your cable TV to a more basic package or drop some of the extras from your cell phone plan. Maybe you need to put in some overtime at work or consider a part-time second job.

The next step is to plan your fiscal month. On your budget worksheet, list your bills in order by due date and assign dates for other expenses (like taking out your cash each Sunday). If you get paid once a month, your fiscal month starts on that date. For example, if your paycheck comes on the 15th of each month, it has to cover all your expenses from the 16th of this month to the 15th of next month. If you get paid twice a month or biweekly, then you have to split your bills in half; you may need to call certain companies and ask them to adjust your due dates to even things out. Try to get far enough ahead that you can afford to pay everything at the beginning of each month.

You should prepare your budget at least a month in advance. If you don't have all your bills for the next month yet, use your best estimate. Then, as you go through the month, fill in the "Actual Amount" column and add any unexpected expenses that come up. Save your receipts, review your bank statements, and check your account through your bank's website. You don't want to lose track of what you're spending and end up overdrawing your account.

Credit and Debt

For many people, part of the monthly budget is devoted to paying off debt: credit cards, mortgage, personal loans, car financing, student loans, and so forth. For the sake of your finances, not to mention your sanity, you should try to have as few outstanding debts as possible and keep current on all the payments.

Student Loans

For most people, higher education is the second-largest expenditure they ever make (after purchasing a home). Because tuition is so expensive, most people cannot afford to pay cash and must take out student loans. If you have student loans, they are a very serious responsibility. Most student loans are government loans, which means that you must pay them back even if you declare bankruptcy. Your postsecondary education is valuable, and your obligation to pay back the loans that financed it is very important. You need to put your student loan payments front and center on your budget, and if you get into trouble with your budget, you need to call your student loan servicer right away to work out a payment plan. The servicer will typically work with you, as long as you stay in communication and sincerely work on making payments.

Credit Cards

The most widespread type of consumer debt is credit card debt. If you charge only what you can afford and pay off your balance each month, a credit card can be a very convenient way of paying for things. Now that many cards offer incentives such as cash back on purchases, you can even come out ahead. The trouble begins when you don't pay off everything you charge each month. When you carry a balance, it's subject to the card's annual percentage rate (**APR**)—a charge that the company imposes on your account and that compounds (or grows)

over time. APRs run from below 10 percent to 30 percent or more, depending on the company and your own credit rating. A 20 percent APR means that for each dollar you owe, you'll be charged 20 cents a year. In one month you'll be charged one-twelfth of that—about 1.66 cents. That may not seem like much, but it adds up. If you carry a balance of $500 for a year, it'll cost you an extra $100.

> ### Financial **Tip**
> Do you know what your credit card APR is? Check your statement.

The average American credit card holder carries about $10,000 in credit card debt, racking up thousands of dollars in finance charges each year. You don't get anything at all for that money, except the privilege of carrying a big chunk of debt. The longer you delay payment, the bigger your balance grows. In the meantime, your minimum monthly payment keeps growing, because it's linked to your balance.

If you're carrying balances on multiple credit cards, you may benefit from consolidating all of them into one account. Many companies offer special promotional rates for balance transfers from other accounts. For instance, they may charge you only 2 percent interest on your transferred balance. Just remember, though, that your regular APR still applies to the balance that is already on your card and to any new purchases. The big advantage to consolidating is that you have to make only one monthly payment, instead of two or three or more.

Credit Reports

You've probably heard about your **credit report** and your **credit score**—mysterious numbers that control your financial life. A credit report is a list of all the credit and utility accounts, loans, collections, and public records (such as court judgments or bankruptcies) in your recent history (generally going back about seven years). Each account's status is reported month by month—whether you paid on time, whether the account is in good standing, how much you owe, and for a closed account, whether it was closed at your request or the company's. The credit score is a number on the report that reflects the estimated level of risk a creditor would take on by lending to you, based on that full history.

Financial **Tip**

Did you know you can get a free copy of your credit report at www.annualcreditreport.com?

When you apply for credit, the financial institution is likely to review your credit report. Based on what it sees, it will choose to approve or deny your request. The report will also be used to determine the interest rate and other terms. Prospective landlords or employers may also look at your credit report to assess your reliability.

Many companies advertise that they can give you access to your credit report, clean up a bad credit history, and beef up your credit score.

There are a few important things to know about credit reports and scores:

You don't have just one. In the United States there are three major credit bureaus— private agencies that compile data from your credit history. Their names are Equifax®, Experian®, and TransUnion®. It's very common for different information to show up on each report. Some lenders will look only at one of the reports; others will check all three.

Name: **Smith, Robert**
Address: **123 Anywhere Street**
City/State/ZIP: **Anytown, IL 55555**

Report #: **46662827**   Report Date: **5/31/11**

Summary

Check to see that your name, current address, former address, and date of birth are correct.
The credit summary gives you a broad look at your current and past credit status. Here you'll find the total number of closed and open accounts in your name, the total balance on those accounts, whether you have any delinquencies, and the number of inquiries made into your credit file.

Account Type/ Bureau	Number of Accounts	Reported Balace	Payments	Current	Closed
Credit Line XPN	1	$5685.09	$95.82	1	0
Installment XPN	2	$20,408.00	$382.94	2	0
Mortgage XPN	0	$0.00	$0.00	0	0
Open XPN	4	$56,978.00	$0.00	0	4
Revolving XPN	9	$18,544.00	$0.00	7	2

Figure 11.3 Credit report sample

You have the right to see your data. Many companies, including the credit bureaus themselves, offer a "free three-in-one credit report"—so long as you sign up for additional "credit protection" services that will cost you a monthly fee. However, federal law gives you the right to one free copy a year of each of your credit reports, no strings attached. Take advantage of this opportunity to review your credit reports for accuracy. To request copies, go to AnnualCreditReport.com, the site officially approved by the Federal Trade Commission.

You have the right to challenge them. Inaccurate information gets into credit reports all the time, and sometimes it can seriously damage your credit. If you find a mistake, you can file a dispute with the bureau, including any supporting evidence or documentation. The bureau is required by law to follow up with the company in question. If the company can't prove its case, or if it doesn't respond, the item must be removed.

You can't fool them. People try to beat the system by challenging every negative mark on their report, even if it's accurate, hoping that not all of the reporting companies will respond. This is, of course, dishonest and unethical. Beyond that, it doesn't work. Eventually, the company will report your debt again—causing a blow to your credit when you least expect it. Don't trust any company that promises to boost your credit score or scrub your report. The only way to improve your credit score is to make your payments on time and avoid getting in over your head.

Identity Theft

Identity theft is a crime in which somebody hijacks your name and credit for his or her own use, potentially leaving your financial affairs in ruins. Identity thieves operate by acquiring some important piece of personal information, such as a credit card number, Social Security number, or computer password, and then commit various frauds, using the stolen identity. A thief may open a credit card account with the stolen identity or use the victim's name to set up a bank account that is then used to write bad checks.

> **It's almost impossible to be completely safe from identity theft, but there are some simple things you can do to minimize your risk:**

Guard your Social Security number. Avoid giving it out if you can, and don't carry your Social Security card in your wallet or purse.

Guard your passwords and PINs. Change computer passwords often, and don't use real words. Make it something you can remember, so that you don't have to write it down. Don't write down your ATM card PIN.

Guard your credit card. Use your card only with merchants you trust. When shopping online, look for sites that offer secure transactions. Avoid giving your credit card number over the phone.

Report theft promptly. If you lose your wallet or if it is stolen, immediately call all the companies necessary to have your credit, debit, and ATM cards canceled and replaced with new ones (with new numbers).

Investing

The financial world offers many opportunities to put your money to work for you, be it through stocks, bonds, mutual funds, or other financial instruments. Investing is no longer just for Wall Street tycoons. Today more people are involved in some kind of investing than ever before. Just remember: Every investment carries risk.

Where to Start

Investing can be very complicated. If you're interested, you should start out small and be cautious. Don't invest more money than you can afford to lose, and expect to pay a price for learning the ropes.

A rule of thumb for all investors is to **diversify,** which means to not put all your eggs in one basket. If you own stock in only one company or industry, you'll lose everything if it tanks. Spread your bets around. A good place to start may be with a mutual fund, in which you join a large group of investors in pooling your resources into a diversified portfolio that has been created by experts.

Some brokerage and investment companies offer entry-level accounts that don't require costly buy-ins. Using an online brokerage will be much less expensive than working with a personal stockbroker, although of course you'll have to make more decisions for yourself. If you have a good deal of money to invest and want to make sure you do it wisely, consider working with a professional financial planner. If you have friends or relatives who are experienced at investing, listen to their advice—but don't let them talk you into taking a bigger risk than you're ready for.

Getting the Most from Your Employee Benefits

In a job search, salary is obviously a top concern. It is also important, though, to be aware of the other kinds of compensation that different employers offer.

Medical Insurance

If your employer offers a health insurance plan, it's probably a better deal than you could get by buying a policy on your own. Group plans have lower premiums, and your employer will usually pay part of yours. Whatever is left of the monthly premium is taken straight from your paycheck, so you don't have to think about it—and it's deducted *before* taxes are calculated, so you don't pay taxes on that money. Generally, a group plan also offers greater security than a private plan. A good employer-provided health insurance plan can add thousands of dollars a year to the value of your total compensation.

Retirement Security

Some employers—particularly those with unionized workforces—offer their employees a **retirement plan** that is designed to provide workers with a stable income after retirement. This is increasingly uncommon, however; most workers are expected to build their own reserves for retirement—and you'll want to start as early as possible, even if you're only in your twenties. Many employers who don't offer pensions still offer some retirement benefits. The best known of these is the 401(k) investment plan. Basically, a 401(k) allows you to invest pre-tax dollars from your pay in a wide range of stocks, funds, and other instruments. Most plans offer the option of building your own portfolio or picking from a series of ready-made ones designed by experts. You don't have to pay taxes on the value of your 401(k) account until you start withdrawing funds from it, after you retire. That allows your money to grow tax-free for decades.

One of the most valuable things about 401(k) plans is that many employers offer "matching" contributions to your account, up to a certain limit. For instance, your employer might make a contribution of up to 3 percent

ON THE JOB

SCENARIO: You've been getting health insurance through your spouse's employer, but your spouse gets laid off. Both of you have pre-existing health conditions, making it difficult to buy affordable private insurance, and you've already declined your employer's health coverage.

QUICK FIX: There are laws in place to protect you. You can choose to continue your existing coverage through your spouse's employer for up to 18 months, although you'll have to pay the full premium. Or you could notify your employer of your spouse's job loss as a "life event," which will allow you to sign up for your employer's health plan in the middle of the year, even though you previously declined it.

of your total pay, provided you contribute at least that much yourself. Another retirement plan is the 403(b). This option is available to employees of educational institutions and certain nonprofit organizations, such as some medical facilities, libraries, and schools. Taxes are paid on earnings from investments (annuities, mutual funds, etc.) after the money is taken out (usually at retirement).

Workplace **Tip**

Many 401(k) or similar plans offer ready-made investment choices based on how long you have to go until retirement. Plans for younger workers focus on higher-risk, higher-yield instruments such as stocks, because there's plenty of time for the young contributor to recover from losses. Older workers' plans are weighted toward safer, lower-yield choices such as government bonds, because they'll be needing to use their money sooner and won't have as much time to make up for any serious losses.

Other Employee Services

While medical and retirement **benefits** are the big-ticket items, some employers offer many other services, including the following:

- Dental insurance
- Vision insurance
- Confidential counseling services
- Pre-tax Flexible Spending Accounts for health care or dependent care expenses
- Health club membership
- Travel agent services
- Transportation credits
- Discounts on company products
- Financial planning
- Legal advice

Depending on your particular lifestyle and needs, these benefits can add up to a lot of value for you.

KAPLAN
success STORY

Michael Earl Ball

El Paso, Texas

Attended: Career Centers of Texas—El Paso, Texas
Area of study: Electrical Technician

Managing your finances is about balancing. I have to work together as a team with my other half. We think about what we need and what we want. We look at the whole list and always pay what we need first. What we want goes onto another list. If we have money after paying what we need, then we get what we want. If not, we try to put money aside each month toward the items on that list.

Unit Summary

- By calculating your monthly expenses against your income and by budgeting in advance, you can take control of your daily financial life.

- Wise use of credit can make your life more convenient, but taking on more than you can pay back will compound your money problems.

- Investing cautiously in a diverse portfolio can help build wealth, but you must be willing to live with risk.

- Employee benefits such as medical insurance and retirement plans can add thousands of dollars to the total value of your compensation at work.

TO-DO List

✔ Practice cutting expenses by skipping an indulgence for a week: dinner out, afternoon snacks, expensive coffee, or something else you regularly spend money on but don't need. Use your Spending Diary to calculate how much you saved in a week, and make an honest assessment about whether it was worth it.

✔ The next time you get a credit card offer in the mail, take the time to read all of the fine print, especially the standard **APR.** Get in the habit of doing this, to develop a sense of which companies really offer the best deals.

✔ Visit your bank's website and see if it offers a low-cost, entry-level investment account.

Important Terms

How well do you know these terms? Look them up in the glossary if you need help remembering them.

APR   credit score

benefits   diversify

budget   identity theft

credit report   retirement plan

Online Resources

About.com's Guide to Financial Planning
http://financialplan.about.com

Identity Theft Information
www.ftc.gov/bcp/edu/microsites/idtheft

Information on Credit Reports
www.ftc.gov/bcp/edu/pubs/consumer/credit/cre34.shtm

Free Annual Credit Report
www.annualcreditreport.com

Exercises

Write your answers on a separate piece of paper.

1. Create a personal budget for next month. Using the monthly budget worksheet on page 149, write down all your expenses and paydays. Track your actual spending by using your Spending Diary, and revise your budget as needed for the following month.

2. Go online and research opportunities for beginning investors. Start with a simple Internet search for "entry-level investing." Write several paragraphs on the types of opportunities that are available and which ones you are most interested in.

3. Many banks offer the convenience of debit cards. Using your bank or the Internet for reference, describe the differences between debit cards and credit cards. When might you use one rather than the other? Which one is safer?

4. Go to your student portal and take the Money Management for Students quiz.

UNIT

12

Career
Development

Understanding the keys to reliability and how they can give you an advantage

Forming productive relationships with co-workers, collaborators, and peers

Remaining flexible in changing circumstances

Developing a healthy attitude toward adversity and practicing techniques for staying positive

Developing a career plan by deciding where you want to be in the future

i t used to be that an employee would work for one company for his or her entire career and retire with a nice pension, but times have changed. Today, employees are far more mobile, changing jobs every four to five years, and companies are far more flexible, making frequent changes that require reorganizations and layoffs. It is an important aspect of professionalism to take career development into your own hands and save for your own retirement. Truly great companies and supervisors take employee development seriously and will be active partners in helping you build your career. However, even if your company or your boss does not have terrific career development resources, you can still reach your goals if you follow the steps in this unit.

The Keys to Reliability

Remember the EDGE? In Unit 10, we discussed the *E*'s (Empowered and Engaged) in depth. The other two Pillars of Professionalism are Dependable and Goal-Oriented, which are the keys to reliability. If you are seen as reliable at work, you will have access to above-average raises, opportunities for advancement, and positive references when you leave the company. You can obtain these very valuable rewards by proving every day at work that you are dependable and goal-oriented.

Being Responsible

Being responsible to your job and your growing career means thinking ahead.

> **You should think beyond merely performing assigned tasks and consider the following actions:**

Be punctual. Always show up on time—for work, for meetings, even for casual occasions like office birthday celebrations. Build a reputation as someone who is always there, always reliable, in every situation. If you have trouble with punctuality, create a Time Management Plan. There is a good template in Unit 13.

Meet your deadlines. Accomplish all your assigned tasks—early, if you can. Do them well: Treat each responsibility, however trivial or low-level it may seem, as if it were the most important task you could imagine. How you handle the little things is a big part of what forms your professional image. You want your boss to know that you'll do a good job on whatever you're asked to do, not cut corners because something seems unimportant or because you don't like that kind of work.

Being Accountable

Being responsible at work means not only doing your work, but also being accountable for its quality. Broadly speaking, **accountability** means that you assume responsibility for the consequences of your own actions.

Don't blame. If you fail to complete a task, if you come in late, or if something goes wrong with your work product, be prepared to explain why you fell short and how you'll ensure that it won't happen again. If you were hurt by circumstances beyond your control, say so—but say so simply. Don't make elaborate excuses for yourself, and don't blame others.

Learn from your mistakes. Always stay focused on the positive and on the future. Own up to what's already happened, and then move on to the things you can control—namely, what you will do next.

Showing Initiative

A person who shows initiative thinks about things that need to be done and gets started on those tasks in advance of being told.

> **Here are some tips for being perceived as goal-oriented, or as a person who shows initiative:**

Think ahead. Every employee's tasks help the overall organization meet its goals. Ask yourself, how does your current task help the larger organization? Are there other things you can do to help with achieving this larger goal? What are the next steps after your current task? Can you begin preparing now for the things you'll be asked to do later? If you can think about what will come next and can get going on it before your boss asks you to, you will be recognized as being goal-oriented. That is one of the most important signs of professionalism identified by employers. Your boss will be very excited if you can figure out what he or she needs next without even being asked.

Support your team. What are your co-workers doing to work toward shared goals? How does their work affect your tasks, and vice versa? Are there ways you can help out or team up? If you can show initiative by helping co-workers, you can kill two birds with one stone—you will be recognized for being goal-oriented, and you will be building a positive relationship with your co-workers. Do be careful to communicate what you are doing, however. If you guess wrong, you may go in the wrong direction. Clear communication should keep you on the right track. Just ask your co-workers if your doing this extra work would be helpful, before you start doing it.

Learn on the job. The regular workday provides many opportunities to learn new skills and processes. Try to take advantage of them. Get out front when special projects come up. If a co-worker is out for an extended absence, volunteer to take on some of his or her duties temporarily. Be on the lookout for people with specialized duties who are looking to train a backup. If a task requires you to collaborate with someone from a different group, pay attention to his or her part of the work; take the opportunity to ask about what your co-workers do. People who do not have initiative avoid extra work and hide when someone is out sick; workers who are goal-oriented see extra work as an opportunity to build new skills and get ahead.

Remember, always do your assigned tasks first. You don't want to get so busy with big-picture thinking that you become distracted from your basic assigned tasks, but combining solid fundamentals with big-picture thinking will make a huge difference in whether you're seen as just a hired hand or as a valuable asset with potential.

Being Flexible

The world is changing at a dizzying pace, and this kind of rapid change will affect your professional life. Over the course of your career, you'll see many changes, including technological and organizational changes. Although you can't control the pace of technology or the global economy, you do have control over your reaction to change. The ability to be flexible in changing circumstances is one of the most valued qualities in the workforce. Employers value flexibility because having an adaptable staff makes the organization itself better able to adapt and remain competitive in a changing environment.

> ### Practice Critical Thinking
>
> Think about some of the things you need to do this week, either in school or at work. How do those tasks fit into a larger purpose? How can you prepare now for tasks you'll be asked to do later on?

ON THE JOB

SCENARIO: Your employer has just reported a second straight quarter of disappointing profits. Word comes down that the main office is planning to close a branch, and yours looks like a top candidate. Morale plummets as people are worrying about losing their jobs—which of course causes productivity to drop at the worst possible time.

QUICK FIX: You talk with the co-workers you have good relationships with. You share concerns but quickly move the conversation into positive territory. You suggest putting together a group to brainstorm ways to improve performance and morale. Just by trying, you may feel better. You may actually perform better, and you could also get noticed and earn future consideration when changes come. What's more, you show yourself to be a strong leader.

Attitude is often as important as expertise when you are facing change. The benefit of maintaining a **positive attitude** is twofold: First, it's easier to learn something new—whether it's a new procedure at work or an upgrade to a software program—when you go into it with an open mind and a positive attitude. Second, your employer will appreciate it. When unexpected things happen—and they do, frequently—employers value versatile employees who can take them in stride, all the while maintaining a positive attitude. If you are asked to take on a new responsibility or learn a new procedure, be flexible and look at it as a welcome opportunity to show your employer how adaptable you are.

The Steps to Building Your Career Development Plan

There is only one person who can ensure that your career keeps moving forward. You guessed it: you. You are the person who cares the most whether you get jobs that are increasingly more interesting, whether you get roles that make more and more money, and whether you get the kind of flexibility and freedom that comes with advancement. These things won't happen by themselves. You need to make a plan and work to make them happen.

Here are the important steps:

1. **Get real about how the world works.** Before you start building your **career development plan,** you need to have the right attitude. We all know that the work world is neither perfect nor fair. Some employees react to this by rebelling—complaining that they should be promoted, chafing at the assignments they are given—instead of looking at their careers as a game that they can learn how to play.

Some jobs make more than others. Many employees seem to think that raises and bonuses are about whether the boss likes them. They charge into their supervisor's office and demand more money, saying that they are worth it! Well, we are all worth it, but unfortunately that isn't how most of the world works. The way it works in a capitalist system is that certain jobs pay certain rates, based on the local market (including concepts like supply and demand). Receptionists tend to make less than executive assistants. Medical assistants tend to make less than nurses. Apprentices tend to make less than union plumbers. New corrections officers make less than 20-year veterans. Unless you win the lottery, you're going to have to make your money with hard work. Although it isn't fair, some job categories make more money than others. Jobs that are close to revenue (i.e. sales jobs) tend to pay better, as do jobs that are risky or unpleasant and jobs that require rare skills or high levels of education. If you're curious about what pays well, scan a jobs website like Monster.com and sort by salary.

To get more, you have to do more. Your boss can't just say, "Abra cadabra," and make your pay rate thousands of dollars higher; the organization is built around certain pay scales. If you want to advance, you are going to need to get more education, take on more responsibility, accept harder work, manage more people, work longer hours, or volunteer for tougher hours. There may not be opportunities to advance at your current organization, so you may also need to move to another organization in order to take advantage of your progress. If you haven't done anything to improve your position, then you should consider yourself lucky to get a 2 percent raise each year.

Your job is more than just your boss and your pay rate. When you have a bad day at work, you may feel the desire to quit. Most people who quit do so because they don't like their boss or their pay rate. However, don't be too hasty. A job has many more elements to it than your boss and your pay rate. When you are evaluating a job, consider the whole package—boss, hours, flexibility, job security, pay rate, interesting work, growth opportunities, co-workers, working conditions, benefits, commute, level of respect—because all these features are important aspects of your work experience. If only one of these things is going badly, give yourself a little time to calm down before you make a rash decision.

Be strong in the face of adversity. Work can be tough, and other parts of your life, such as your family or your health, can add to your stress. What's more, any time your company, your industry, or your community goes through rough times, that tension gets passed down to you. You'll find, however, that letting your stress affect you at work only adds to the stress in the long run. Taking out frustration on co-workers or displaying a bad attitude in the office puts a strain on your relationships, makes people less inclined to communicate with you, and tends to put others in a bad mood, too—and they may take it out on you. On a more basic level, it's just unprofessional. Remember that nothing lasts forever. Think about things you can do to help make things easier on yourself and your co-workers, and look ahead to what you'd like to do in the future.

2. Clean your house. Now that you're feeling empowered, make sure your professional house is clean. You can't start the process of career development from behind the starting line. You need to be in good standing at work if you expect to make progress.

Make your employer happy. You may not be in your dream job yet, but do you need a job now in order to build up to the next job. So, make your current boss happy. Follow directions, and try to anticipate what needs to be done. In short, be a professional, and practice your EDGE qualities.

Create a situation in which the company wants to invest in you. Do your best to make yourself valuable to the company. Most companies don't even consider developing employees for the first 6 to 12 months. So, in your first year, it is your job to give to the company. After that, it may consider giving you a raise or expanding your assignments. If you make yourself useful and available, you will increase the chances that the company will invest in you.

Set yourself up for a good performance appraisal. Every organization has its own system for evaluating employees' performance on the job. Some **performance appraisals** occur annually; some happen quarterly, or even more often; and some companies never do them at all. Some have a direct impact on pay, and others are geared more toward coaching and quality improvement. Performance reviews can be stressful, especially if you are worried about your performance. Remember, however, that they are stressful for your manager, too, since he or she knows the review will be in your permanent record. You can set yourself up to win by keeping a regular log of the tasks you complete, the ideas you contribute, and the results you achieve. Think especially in terms of how

what you've done has benefited your department or company. If you can link your accomplishments to the company's profit, be sure to record that. When review time comes, go over all that you've documented and identify the highlights to point out to your manager. Don't be modest; show how valuable you are.

3. Set a goal. You may not know where you want to be five or ten years from now, but go ahead and set a goal anyway. It's okay if your goal changes later. It just helps focus your thinking to have a goal in mind.

Here's how to set one:

Decide what matters to you. Some people are all about money; they just want to make as big a salary as possible. Other people are all about prestige; they don't care about the salary as long as the job gets a lot of respect. Still other people care more about whether the work is interesting or whether it contributes to the environment or whether it helps people. There is no judgment here. Just decide what matters to you. It's all right to keep this information to yourself. Nobody needs to know your goals but you. To give you some ideas, here is a list of things that people find important about their jobs: a nice boss, good work hours, flexibility, job security, a high pay rate, interesting work, growth opportunities, fun co-workers, great working conditions, solid benefits, short commute, a high level of respect. Put your priorities in order.

Find a job description for a job you want. You can look around your company for ideas. Is there someone who has a job you'd really like? It's okay if it's the CEO or Executive Director—there's no problem with dreaming big. It's also just fine if it's at your same level or only one level up. This is your goal. Just make sure it is a job that you would really like to have. You can find job descriptions and even salary ranges on job websites like

CareerBuilder.com or Monster.com. Keep looking until you find a job posting that you would want. This job description is your goal. You can change your goal whenever you want.

4. **Create a career development plan.**
   Take your goal (the job description) and use it to create a plan for your career. The objective of your plan is to build up all your skills and qualifications, so that you could apply for your dream job and have a reference to sign off on every skill and qualification.

Workplace **Tip**

When you're preparing for a performance appraisal, think about the accomplishments that meant the most, not just to you, but to your organization. It's important to link your achievements to the company's overall success.

Cross off the skills and qualifications you already have. Go through the points in the job description, and cross off the qualifications that you already have—those for which you have a reference who could say, "Yes, this skill exists in this person and is solid." For example, if the job description says *Certification in CPR* and you already have that, cross it off. If it says *Familiar with Microsoft Word* and you can write documents in Microsoft Word®, then cross it off. These are the skills you already have—congratulations!

Of what is left, circle the qualifications that would take a long time to acquire. Some qualifications take a long time to earn. For example, if the job description says *Minimum bachelor's degree required* and you don't have a bachelor's degree yet, circle that, because it usually takes longer than two years to acquire a bachelor's degree.

Identify the skills and qualifications you could acquire on your current job. Of the skills and qualifications that are left (neither crossed off nor circled), some of them could probably be performed on your current job. If you have a good boss, ask if it might be possible to practice some of these skills. Even if they are not exactly on your job description, a good boss will try to work in some of them for you if you ask about them. If you have a tough boss, just see if you can find opportunities to try these skills so you can add them to your resume. Keep a list on hand of the skills you're trying to get, and cross them off as you get them.

Make a plan for acquiring the remaining skills and qualifications. For the circled skills, is it practical to go after one or more of them now? It may not be. Sometimes, you need to pay off your student loans for a bit before you go for another degree, and that's okay. If you can get working on the long-term skills, do so. You'll feel proud that you are making progress. For the other skills, think about the next job you could get where you could practice those skills. Is there a job like that at your company? What other company might have a job like that? The answers will point you toward the next step in your career.

It may seem odd to be making such a long-term career development plan. However, if you don't set a goal and go after it, the chances of your getting it are slim. If you were a basketball player, you would know that 100 percent of the shots you don't take don't go in. You need to take a shot to have the chance to win.

5. **Check in regularly with your mentors.**
   If you have a good boss, you are really fortunate. A manager who cares about your career development is solid gold and can serve as a lifetime mentor. If you don't have a good boss, you will need to use an outside mentor to help you with your career. You

may find a mentor from among the instructors and staff on your Kaplan Higher Education campus. Or, you may find a mentor as you are networking or interviewing during your job search. When you find people who have a lot of experience in your field, ask them if they would be willing to mentor you from time to time. Many of them will be willing to help out. They were at the beginning of their career journeys once, and they know how hard it is to get started. They will want to share what they know and help you out. Take advantage of their willingness to guide you, and ask them to help with your career development plan.

Ron Briney, Jr.
Crafton, Pennsylvania

Attended: Kaplan Career Institute—ICM Campus, Pittsburgh, Pennsylvania
Area of study: Information Technology
Employer: Comcast
Position: Advanced Solutions Representative

If you take one thing away from this course, it should be this: I learned that through hard work and sacrifice you can achieve your goals.

Coming to Kaplan saved my life. Everyone at Kaplan treated me very well. They cared, challenged, and dared me to succeed. Every day I had help in many different ways. In my eyes, they didn't come to work for a paycheck; they came to make a difference, and did.

Unit Summary

- For a successful professional, the keys to reliability include being dependable and being goal-oriented.

- Being flexible and willing to adapt to change is essential in the workplace.

- By learning to handle adversity with a positive attitude, you will decrease your stress and be seen as a reliable and level-headed co-worker.

- Take control of your own growth by making a step-by-step Career Development Plan.

- Before you start your Career Development Plan, make sure to understand the workplace "game."

- Gather mentors who can help guide you on your career journey.

TO-DO List

✔ Practice being dependable. List five things that other people are counting on you to do this week, and make sure you do them. Check them off your list when you do them.

✔ Find a job description for a job you would really like to have five years from now.

✔ Do an Internet search on your industry, and see what professional conferences or seminars are available.

Important Terms

How well do you know these terms? Look them up in the glossary if you need help remembering them.

accountability

career development plan

performance appraisal

positive attitude

Online Resources

Career Development
www.ncda.org

Job Descriptions and Salary Information
www.careerbuilder.com
www.monster.com

Exercises

Write your answers on a separate piece of paper.

1. Begin developing a long-term career plan by writing several paragraphs about where you'd like to be in five, ten, and fifteen years. Consider not just job titles but also family and personal goals.

2. As practice for a future evaluation by a supervisor, create a short performance appraisal for yourself. The appraisal can apply to your performance as a student, or it can apply to your current job if you have one. Think about your work over the past six to twelve months and list what you think are your five greatest strengths and weaknesses; three or four of your best achievements; three or four things you'd like to learn more about; and two or three objectives for your work over the next year.

3. Using the job description you found in the To-Do List exercise, follow the steps in this unit to create a Career Development Plan.

Time Management

KEYS TO
success

Assessing your work habits and time usage each week

Prioritizing your weekly tasks and commitments

Identifying commitments and activities that can be sacrificed to make time for your top priorities

Creating a realistic schedule for your personal, professional, and academic activities

Developing effective time management techniques

Recognizing that life rarely proceeds exactly as planned

i t's the night before the big test, and you haven't even started studying. You break out the caffeine (coffee, or one of those crazy drinks?), and you reach for the sugar (candy? soda?). Decision time: Are you going to stay up all night? Or, are you just going to wing it?

Our lives are busy, and most of us find that we don't have enough time to do the important things we wish to accomplish. Running out of time to study for a test, however, can have serious consequences. Cognitive scientists have proven that cramming for a test is not as effective as spacing out your study over time (Kornell, 2009).[1] If you let it get down to the wire, you will learn less, and it could affect your work performance later. The solution to this problem is time management, and in this unit, we will show you how to plan and prioritize so that you have enough time for your work—and for some fun, as well.

[1] Kornell, N. (2009). Optimising learning using flashcards: Spacing is more effective than cramming. *Applied Cognitive Psychology,* 23(9), 1297–1317. doi 10.1002/acp.1537

Take Control of Your Time

One day you open up the newspaper and see an article about someone you knew in high school who is now a successful business owner. You remember this guy as one of the biggest goof-offs in school. The two of you started in the same place, at the same time. How did he get so far ahead of you? The answer isn't what he did year by year; it's what he did hour by hour. Nobody has more than 24 hours in a day. Successful people make the most of their time.

If you want to take the next step in your career—and also have a rewarding life outside of work and school—you'll have to start making the most of your 24 hours each day. Easier said than done, right? It seems as if there's always so much more to do than you have time for. The first thing to do is take an inventory of your time and activities.

Assessing Your Day

Certain features of your day are non-negotiable: your work hours, your class schedule, the amount of sleep you need to make it through the day. Not having enough time can be frustrating, but it's the reality you face, so there's no point in getting stressed over it. When your paycheck comes, you know a chunk has been taken out for taxes, but you don't think much about that; you plan what you're going to do with the *net*—the amount actually *in* your check. Consider time in the same way: Just think about your after-tax, "net" day.

Taking Stock of Your Goals

Now, think about your goals. Work backward until you reach the first step that you can take right away. In a typical week, you'll try to make measurable progress toward a few short-term goals while keeping sight of your intermediate and long-term goals.

Make a list of everything you *have* to accomplish this week, such as completing an assignment for class, paying your utility bills, or getting an oil change for your car. Then review your less pressing goals, and figure out the next steps toward achieving each of them.

Personal Time

Take a look at your other obligations for the week, such as going to a birthday dinner for your sister, helping your friend set up his new computer, or coaching the Little League team. If you have a heavy load of personal commitments this week, accept that you won't get as far toward accomplishment of your goals. That's fine; in fact, it's essential to keep a healthy life balance.

Finally, make sure you think about what you *want* to do this week. If you can't afford to spend an hour in the evening sitting on the couch watching Letterman, or join in the Halo® video game tournament Friday night, or go to the mall on Saturday afternoon, then you'll find yourself resenting the goals you have set. This will only make you more likely to drop them.

Setting Priorities

The next step is to assign priorities to all the things you need and want to do this week. Rank them, from top to bottom, in the following order:

- Things you have no control over: paying the bills, putting gas in the car
- Things you can do now that will spare you time or stress later: keeping up on your coursework rather than cramming the night before a test
- Things that need to be done eventually but can be postponed without becoming harder or more time-consuming: doing laundry, washing your car

Your personal priorities will mix in with these. Some things you have to do, such as celebrating your sister's birthday (think of all the time you'd have to spend to make up for missing it). Then there are the little things you look forward to every day that make you feel it's all worthwhile: spending time with your family or significant other, running in the park in the morning, having coffee with your friends after work. Make sure your schedule includes time for the small things that you really enjoy.

Also assess your personal priorities according to how much you will regret *not* doing something. For instance, if that Halo tournament is your only chance to see an old buddy visiting from out of town, that makes it more important than a regular evening sitting in the basement playing video games.

Time Management **Tip**

Setting priorities helps you decide which tasks are most pressing. If you have only two hours free on Sunday afternoon, you may have to choose between watching a DVD rental and studying for your pharmacology exam. You'll find that you may have to set aside one or more tasks to achieve the others. In this way, planning involves setting priorities.

Creating a Time Management Plan

If there is one message you should take away from this unit, it is this: You must have a detailed **time management plan** outlining the things you need to do each day. If you don't, you'll wind up at the end of the day wondering where all the time went.

The most common reason people don't prepare time management plans is that it's just too intimidating. Looking at your obligations for a given week all at once can be discouraging. What's more discouraging, though, is to leave it all up to chance. Then you may end up putting off half of your tasks until the next week, which, combined with that week's duties, will leave you facing an even bigger mountain.

Assessing Your Habits

Nothing shows the benefits of having a plan better than the results of having no plan. For a week, track how you spend your time. Draw up a grid for the week on paper, with a box for writing down what you do and how long it takes, starting when you normally get up in the morning and ending when you go to bed. Carry the grid with you at all times. Fill it in at least twice a day—at lunch and before you go to bed—and write down everything you've done during the day.

Be brutally honest. Don't report that you were studying from 7:00 p.m. to 10:00 p.m. if you got sidetracked by instant messages

Monday	
7:00–7:30	got up, showered
7:30–8:00	ate breakfast, checked email
8:00–8:30	got ready for class, organized books and supplies for the day, finished Unit 4 exercises
8:30–9:00	drove to school
9:00–12:00	attended class
12:00–1:30	had lunch with Tamantha
1:30–2:00	drove home
2:00–3:30	watched TV, read blogs online, checked email, organized and paid bills, did laundry
3:30–3:45	got ready for work
3:45–4:00	drove to work
4:00–6:00	worked
6:00–6:30	ate dinner
6:30–10:00	worked
10:00–10:15	drove home
10:15–11:00	ate snack, watched TV, checked email
11:00–12:00	finished part of Unit 5 reading assignment

Figure 13.1 Sample grid with daily activities tracked

at 8:30 p.m. and didn't get back to work until 9:00 p.m. Did you really work until 6:00 p.m., or did you get off at 5:30 p.m. and spend half an hour talking to co-workers before heading home?

At the end of the week, check your grid for these red flags:

Time wasters. Did you devote big blocks of time to watching TV, reading blogs online, or talking on the phone? There's nothing wrong with any of these activities, but they have no specific goal or ending point. It's easy to keep going until your whole evening is gone— even though you may have intended to spend only half an hour.

Long time blocks. If you spent three hours or more on one task, ask yourself what you accomplished in that time, and if the product was worth the time you put into it. If you had allowed yourself an hour less for the task and really worked at it, could you have made the same amount of progress? If you reach a point where you feel as if you're getting nowhere, take a break or move on to something else. Come back later, when you can start with a new frame of mind.

Practice
Critical Thinking
Think about how you spend your time during a typical week. Which of the pitfalls described above are the biggest challenges for you? What are some strategies you can try to help you waste less time?

Gaps. Are there spaces on your grid showing times when you were sitting idle between one scheduled job and the next? Half an hour isn't enough time to do anything, right? Wrong. There are probably a dozen small tasks you could have completed in that time and crossed off your list.

Building Your Schedule

Now that you have a record of how you actually spend your time, look for ways to organize your day more efficiently. Draw up a new grid, and start filling it out by listing your tasks and goals for the week. This allows you to budget your time and helps you balance your activities. Without a schedule, you can end up spending all your time on the top priorities and neglecting the items that are lower on the list but are still very important. For instance, if you're working on a class project, you could continue to tinker and try to make it better forever if you so desired. A schedule will provide a cutoff point at which you decide enough is enough and move on to other things.

A schedule also helps you split your time between **"hard" obligations**—commitments with specific deadlines or due dates—and **"soft" obligations** over which you have more control. If you don't allow time for your soft tasks, they will always get squeezed out by the hard ones.

Setting the Bar

Keep your expectations high, but be realistic. A schedule you can't meet is no better than no schedule at all—and can be even worse, because of the discouragement that comes at the end of the week when you realize you haven't done half the things you meant to do.

When you achieve specific goals, you engage your brain's reward center; this is what makes you feel so good. Crossing an item off your to-do list gives you the same feeling as sinking a shot on the basketball court or reaching a new level on a video game.

It is also a good idea to reward yourself for taking care of business. You'll be more motivated

Monday	
7:00–7:30	get up, shower
7:30–7:45	check email
7:45–8:00	eat breakfast
8:00–8:30	organize and pay bills, get ready for class
8:30–9:00	drive to school
9:00–12:00	attend class
12:00–1:00	have lunch with Tamantha
1:00–1:30	drive home
1:30–2:00	watch TV, relax
2:00–3:30	do laundry, finish Unit 5 reading assignment and exercises
3:30–3:45	get ready for work
3:45–4:00	drive to work
4:00–6:00	work
6:00–6:30	eat dinner, review exercises and unit vocabulary
6:30–10:00	work
10:00–10:15	drive home
10:15–11:00	check and answer email, relax
11:00–11:30	organize books and supplies for tomorrow

Figure 13.2 Sample grid with daily tasks planned

to finish your income tax return if you make plans to kick back and watch an eagerly anticipated movie when you're done. Nothing feels better than relaxing and doing what you like once you can say to yourself, "I've earned it."

Making Sacrifices

You can't create a workable schedule simply by cutting out inefficiencies. To achieve your goals, you'll have to make some sacrifices.

You've taken the first step by prioritizing your needs, wants, and commitments. Now you have to make some hard choices. Think about the amount of time you spend on a particular task, and consider whether it's a good investment. Coaching the Little League team is a hard and fast commitment: You have to show up for several hours every Saturday, period. But there are a lot of other things you could do with your weekend time. Some are so important to you that you attend to them during the week—but that cuts into your scheduled time for study or other obligations. You have to ask yourself if the coaching gig is something you can afford the time for right now. You can't do everything you might want to do. That's just a fact of life.

Tools for Time Management

Many different tools and methods can be used to put together a schedule. Different ways work best for different people; the important thing is to convert your time management program from a mental construction to a physical form you can actually look at and use to hold yourself accountable.

First of all, there's nothing wrong with using paper. For a grid you fill in by hand, you can either draw up a new grid every week with a pencil and a ruler or print a blank grid from a computer. The advantage of using paper is that you can carry it with you anywhere. You can stick it on your refrigerator door or on the wall next to your work area. You can update it just by reaching over and marking it. Filling everything in by hand can be time-consuming, but if it makes your schedule more accessible to you, it's worth it.

On the other hand, your computer offers many useful time management tools, which are loaded with convenient features. There is probably a basic calendar program built into the operating system; look for it under "Accessories." Some email programs, such as Microsoft Outlook®, have built-in calendars for entering appointments and tasks. If you use a free web-based email service, such as Gmail™, it may also offer an online calendar. You can also build your own by using a spreadsheet program, such as Microsoft Excel. Most "smart phones," such as the BlackBerry® or the iPhone®, offer an electronic calendar that you can carry on the go. Just don't get caught up in playing with these devices for half an hour every time you go to check your appointments.

In addition to storing your schedule, many software programs allow you to build a to-do

Time Management **Tip**

Try not to get distracted by interruptions such as phone calls, text messages, and personal emails. Although a ringing phone may seem to demand your immediate attention, chances are you can take the call later with no penalty. Unless the call concerns something truly urgent, plan to respond later if you are in the middle of a task. Designate a certain time for checking and answering email, rather than being distracted by checking your email every 15 minutes.

list. A to-do list, prepared each morning or the night before, lists all the tasks you want to accomplish that day. The very act of creating the list helps in planning your day and strengthening your commitment. With some programs, you set a due date for a task, and the program alerts you when it's approaching. Combining your calendar with a **task list** can be of great help in tracking your goals and making the most of your time.

Of course, if you're computer-shy or can't afford all the bells and whistles, low-tech solutions are just as good. Try writing down each of your tasks for the week on an index card.

Whenever you find yourself with a chunk of free time—whether it's 15 minutes or an hour—shuffle through the stack of cards until you find something you can accomplish in the time you have. Update the cards as you make progress, and put the completed ones in a separate pile.

You can also use a planner to create a to-do list for daily activities. Planners are calendars designed for listing daily tasks. Your planner should be your sole source of information about your schedule. Use it to record and schedule all commitments of your time and keep it up to date.

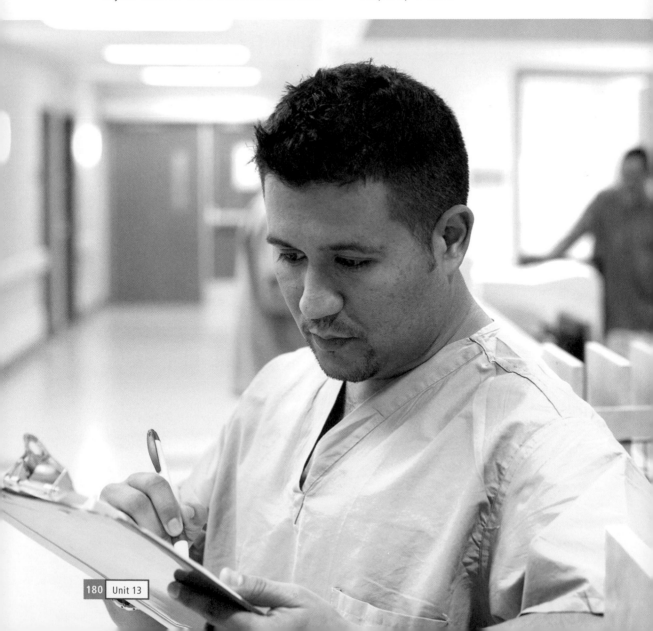

Making an Impact with Your Time Management

In the professional workplace and in school, the difference between people who manage their time well and those who don't is crystal clear. Setting priorities, understanding which tasks need to be done first, and having a plan to complete all of them allows you to stay on top of your obligations. By staying organized and using your time efficiently, you keep yourself prepared for the unexpected. Good time managers rise to challenges, roll with changes, and seize opportunities. They command respect and inspire confidence. They're given greater responsibility in their jobs. Greater responsibility means they get to learn more, which makes them stronger candidates for promotion and gives them an advantage in the job market.

Poor time managers, on the other hand, struggle to keep up with their basic duties, have trouble communicating with superiors, and often have difficulty accepting change. They show up for class unprepared and often late. Co-workers learn not to count on them, and when special projects are in the works, they're left out. Because they are poor job candidates, they live in fear of losing the jobs they have, which puts them at the mercy of their superiors. If you don't learn to take control of your time on the job, you may wind up putting in a lot of extra hours doing work of doubtful quality.

Time Management **Tip**

Sometimes you can't say no to a demanding boss. If you are overcommitted at work and your boss asks you to take on additional responsibilities, don't refuse. Instead, briefly outline your current responsibilities and ask your boss for help balancing your competing priorities.

Learning to Prioritize

There are only so many hours in a day. The effective time manager knows this. Assuming you have a reasonable boss, practice turning down additional projects, responsibilities, or demands when accepting them would mean becoming overcommitted. You need to weigh the demands for your time. Practicing assertiveness and the willingness to prioritize will help you accomplish your tasks and goals on time.

Be Dependable

The best thing you can do to improve or preserve your professional image and job prospects is to be dependable.

Show Up on Time

The primary thing employers must be able to count on is the presence of their employees. If your boss calls an emergency meeting first thing in the morning and you are absent or late, do you want to be the reason he or she has to repeat the information later, or the reason everyone has to wait to receive important information?

ON THE **JOB**

SCENARIO: Your clinical supervisor asked you to finish entering the new patient information in the database by the end of the day. You're halfway done when your co-worker Lisa, who is checking patients in, is forced to go home to handle an emergency. The clinic is very busy and you fill in for Lisa, and consequently there's no way you can get the database updated by the end of the day.

QUICK FIX: Tell your supervisor what happened. Make sure he knows that you had to fill in for Lisa and it wound up taking up most of the afternoon. You need another hour to finish updating the database, and you'll do it first thing tomorrow morning. If it's really important, offer to stay late to finish, so that it will be waiting for the supervisor in the morning.

If your workday or your school day starts at 8:30 a.m., plan to get there by 8:15 a.m. This gives you some wiggle room for any of the countless unpredictable events that could occur on the way to work or to school. If a slow-moving freight train is blocking the road you're on, it's nice to be able to just sit and listen to the radio and not have to worry about how many minutes late you're going to be. Be realistic about how much time you need to get ready in the morning. Is it really worth it to sleep an extra 15 minutes if that means choosing between eating breakfast and making your train?

If you're lucky enough to have "flex" hours at work, you should still pick a start time and stick to it every day. Your boss and co-workers will find it reassuring to know that they can count on your being there. Nothing will damage your image at work more quickly than being known as the person who gets there "whenever."

Meet Your Deadlines

A task with a looming deadline jumps to the top of your priority list. If something has to be done by the end of your shift, make that task a priority when you arrive at work. If a supervisor has to ask you for something twice, you can bet the second time will be less pleasant. Any time you're given a task, ask when it needs to be completed. If there is no deadline, set one for yourself so that you won't forget.

Again, you don't want a superior asking you for something twice.

Keep a list of your most pressing tasks, and their due dates, in the most visible part of your work area—stuck to your computer monitor, in your locker, on your bulletin board, wherever you're most likely to see it—and use it as a helpful reminder.

If a deadline is approaching and you know you're not going to make it, you're obviously not in the best situation—but you can still handle it and maintain your reliability. The first step is to recognize when you're in trouble. Next, provide a status update as early as possible. Take responsibility for the situation, but if there's a good reason why you've fallen behind—for instance, the task turned out to be more complicated than anyone anticipated—report it. Explain it simply, briefly, and calmly. Provide an honest, realistic assessment of when you expect to be finished—and make *sure* you meet that new deadline.

Remember that spending extra time on one task affects all others. If you have to spend an extra day finishing a project for school or for work, make sure to reassess the time set aside for other pressing matters so that you won't be late on them too.

Prepare in Advance

If you really want to get ahead, plan your tasks as far in advance as possible. As soon as you know of an upcoming deadline, a meeting or an event that's just been scheduled, or a project that's coming down the pike, put it on your calendar.

Whenever you have some downtime at home or at work, use it to prepare for tasks you know are coming up. You can get ahead on your reading assignment for class and reduce your workload for next week. At work you can organize the supply cabinet or take inventory of the office supplies. Not only will this make things easier when crunch time comes, but it will also show your supervisor that you take initiative and plan ahead.

The more you know about your future schedule, the better you'll be able to assess how much extra you can take on right now. You want to say yes to as much as possible, but not to things on which you can't deliver.

By taking control of your time at school or on the job, you'll reduce your stress level, boost your performance, and enjoy improved relationships with your boss and co-workers or with your instructors and classmates. Remember, 80 percent of success comes from just showing up, being there when you're needed, and striving to be an asset rather than an obstacle at your workplace.

KAPLAN
success
STORY

Shannon Vargesko
McKeesport, Pennsylvania

Attended: Kaplan Career Institute—ICM Campus, Pittsburgh, Pennsylvania
Area of study: Business Administration Management
Position/Employer: Administrative Assistant to the CFO, YMCA of Greater Pittsburgh

If you take one thing away from this course, it should be this: I do what I can in my eight-hour day, and leave the rest for the next. Prioritizing your responsibilities and staying organized makes this easier to achieve.

Kaplan provided the bridge that guided me to becoming a professional, as well as the opportunity for growth as an individual. Kaplan teachers have real-world experience and tips that they share with their class.

Unit Summary

- The first step toward effective time management is to take a realistic view of how many hours are available in your week. All of your personal, professional, and academic activities should be ranked by priority to identify those that are the most pressing.

- A weekly schedule that accounts for all your time and all your necessary tasks is the core of any successful time management plan.

- A task list can help you keep track of the progress you have made toward your goals.

- People who manage their time well enjoy higher productivity, reduced stress, and better relationships.

TO-DO List

- ✔ Make a list of the five biggest time wasters in your typical week.

- ✔ On your calendar, mark off every day in the next six months that you know is fully or mostly committed and on which you know you won't be able to get anything else done (holidays, family get-togethers, trips, and so forth).

- ✔ Make a list of everything that you know right now you have to do—even if it's as routine as sending an email or making a phone call. Make your best guess as to how long each task will take, and write that next to each one.

- ✔ Practice making sacrifices: Make a list of three things you normally do each week that you are willing to give up.

Important Terms

How well do you know these terms? Look them up in the glossary if you need help remembering them.

hard obligation   **time management plan**

soft obligation   **task list**

Online Resources

Google Calendar
calendar.google.com

Online Time Management, Timesheet, and Time Tracking Tool
www.myhours.com

Templates for Planning Daily and Weekly Activities
office.microsoft.com/en-us/templates/FX100595491033.aspx

Time Management Tips
www.buzzle.com/articles/time-management

Exercises

Write your answers on a separate piece of paper.

1. Create a grid and use it to track all of your activities for a week, using the procedures described in this unit. At the end of the week, go through the grid and circle the spots indicating where you spent time without accomplishing anything or fulfilling any personal needs. Also circle places showing where you spent more time on a task than was useful or worthwhile. Tally up the hours you've singled out.

2. Write a paragraph or two about a time when you accomplished something you set out to do. It can be something big, such as getting a promotion at work, or something smaller, such as cleaning out your closet or saving up for a trip out of town. What made you want to accomplish the goal? What specific steps did you take to do it?

3. Using the techniques outlined in this unit, prepare a weekly schedule for your activities. Block out your time in half-hour segments. Be realistic about how much time you need for sleep, commuting, eating, and other routine activities. Also make sure to allow for enough personal time so that you can continue to do the things you enjoy. After a week, write several paragraphs assessing how closely you stuck to your schedule and noting what changes you think you need to make.

4. Use an Internet search engine, such as Google™, to research time management tools. Look for content as well as software; maybe you can find some blogs with helpful advice. Write a one-page report on the most useful or promising resource you found.

Credits

Glossary

accountability   the state of being held responsible for one's actions

active communication   communication that deliberately conveys something, such as speech, sign language, or gestures

APA style   the format used by the American Psychological Association for citing sources; one of the most commonly used formats in business

application   a form filled out for a potential employer that often requires the same information that appears on a resume or similar information

APR   annual percentage rate; the rate at which finance charges accumulate on a credit account

audience   a group to whom one delivers a presentation; or, the intended readership for a written document

authority   the ability to command the attention of others and influence them, based on recognized expertise

behavioral interview   a type of job interview in which the interviewer asks questions about an applicant's behavior in past work situations, rather than questions about hypothetical situations; for example, "Tell me about a time when you had to prioritize your responsibilities in order to meet a deadline."

benefits   services offered by an employer in addition to salary or wages

bias   a preference or inclination that prevents impartial judgment

blog   short for *weblog;* a personal website that combines the functionality of a daily diary with the ability to post photos and video online; usually offered in a fixed template

brand   a series of ideas, impressions, or feelings about a particular product, company, or person; often identified by a unique slogan, logo, or mark

budget   a detailed plan for managing money

business etiquette   a set of standards for behavior at work that includes showing respect to superiors and co-workers and projecting a professional image

career development plan   a road map of where a person is headed professionally, including where he or she would like to be in five, ten, and fifteen years

chronological resume   a time history of an applicant's work experience, beginning with the most recent position; preferred resume format of many recruiters because it is easy to read

cold lead   information about an available job that is publicly posted by an organization to which the candidate has no connection

confidential   privileged or secret

conflict resolution   the process of ending or minimizing disagreement among groups or individuals, with an emphasis on negotiating to create solutions that take into account the underlying interests and needs of all parties involved

corporate culture   the set of behaviors, values, and attitudes that distinguishes the way an organization pursues its objectives

counteroffer   asking for better terms of employment (higher salary or better benefits, for example) after a job offer has been extended

cover letter   a letter sent with a resume or job application; often tailored to a particular job opening, to provide information about specific skills and qualifications

credit report   a document compiled by a private agency, listing all known information about an individual's payment history on credit accounts, loans, utilities, and other items

credit score   a number on an individual's credit report that estimates the level of risk involved in lending the individual money

culture   a group's particular set of shared rules, customs, values, and assumptions

customer service   the process of preventing conflict relating to the delivery of goods and services and using negotiating skills to resolve conflict when it does arise

digital footprint   information other people can discover about an individual online, both through information he or she posts and through information others post about him or her

diversify   to invest in a broad, balanced portfolio of stocks, bonds, or securities in order to protect against major losses

diversity   the quality of being different; in school or in the workplace, typically refers to the inclusion of people from different races, cultures, and backgrounds

draft   a written document that has not yet undergone revision

EDGE   the Four Pillars of Professionalism: E = Empowered, D = Dependable, G = Goal-Oriented, and E = Engaged

elevator pitch   a short speech or presentation delivered in a minute or less (the length of an elevator ride)

employment agency   a company that matches prospective job candidates with potential employers; may be paid by employers or charge fees to job seekers for its services

ethical behavior   conduct that is in accordance with accepted social and professional standards

ethics   a system for determining moral behavior

exempt employee   an employee who does not get paid by the hour but instead earns a salary

externship   an unpaid work experience available to entry-level job seekers to help them gain knowledge and experience in a particular field

format   the appearance and arrangement of a particular kind of writing

functional resume   a skills-oriented depiction of an applicant's work history; particularly good format for those who are changing careers, have limited paid experience, or have large gaps in employment history

gossip   rumor or sensational talk about others

group interview   an interview format in which the applicant is questioned by a group of people; alternatively, an interview style in which job candidates are interviewed in large groups

hard obligation   a task or commitment with a specific time frame or deadline

headhunter   a professional recruiter who helps people find jobs; often paid by the companies in which they place people

hierarchy the chain of command within an organization, running from the lowest-level employees to the CEO

identity theft a crime in which an individual's name, personal information, or credit is stolen for criminal purposes; can cause damage to the victim's credit and financial standing

illegal behavior conduct that is against the law

intermediate goal an important objective that is achieved over the course of one to three years; usually supports a long-term goal

job fair a sponsored event designed to bring together employers and job candidates in a face-to-face setting

job search wizard an automated way of checking a website to see whether a job has been posted that meets criteria set by a user

keywords one or more words entered into a library catalog or online search engine to find sources on a certain subject

lead information about a possible job opening, or a connection to a person who will be able to provide information about a job opening

leadership the act or quality of providing vision and guidance to an organization or team

letter of recommendation a letter written on behalf of a job applicant, offering an evaluation of the applicant's professional skills and qualifications

long-term goal a significant objective that is achieved over a long period of time (typically several years)

mission statement a written statement detailing the main purpose and direction of a group (such as a company) or an individual

mock interview a practice interview, staged before the actual job interview takes place, that allows an applicant to rehearse answering questions

motivation something that provides incentive to act

narrative a story with a beginning, a middle, and an end; for example, the story told by the documents in your portfolio, reinforcing your image as a person who has accomplished things in the past and has goals and ambitions

networked leads job leads that are acquired through one-on-one conversations; often not publicly posted but typically provided by someone in the organization

networking making connections with professionals who can help in one's career

non-exempt employee an employee who is paid by the hour and is eligible for overtime pay under certain conditions

nonverbal communication aspects of how a person looks and behaves (gestures, clothing, posture, facial expressions, and body language) that communicate information to observers

organizational purpose the larger goals of a department or an employer that motivate the tasks employees perform every day

passive communication communication that conveys information without directly intending or attempting to do so

peers other people with the same or a similar job; other professionals in the same field

perception how a person or entity is generally viewed; often an emotional response

performance appraisal the formal process by which employees are evaluated by their supervisors

personal business   tasks from one's personal life such as paying bills, handling family business, and dealing with social and medical issues that should, as far as possible, be taken care of on one's own time, not at work

personality   the set of behaviors, values, and attitudes that distinguish an individual or a group

plagiarism   the act of using someone else's information, ideas, or words without giving proper credit

policy   a fundamental rule of an individual or organization, either publicly stated or internally known

portfolio   a collection of documents, such as work samples, academic qualifications, and awards, that is designed to provide an overview of professional accomplishments

positive attitude   a mindset that emphasizes being flexible and looking for the good in any situation

Possible Agreement Zone   a range within which both parties in a negotiation would be happy with the outcome

practice interview   see *mock interview*

priority   the level of importance assigned to a task; higher-priority tasks are handled before lower-priority ones

professional development   an activity, such as continuing education, job seminars, or learning on the job, that enhances job skills

reference   in a job search, a person who can provide information about an applicant's personal qualifications and character

resume   a brief written account of an applicant's qualifications, experience, and education, generally sent with or as a job application

retirement plan   an employer-provided benefit that helps an individual build a reserve of income to draw on after retirement

revision   the act of improving an earlier version of a document, including not only correcting spelling and grammar, but also improving focus

reward center   the part of the brain involved with producing the sensation of pleasure

self-assessment   an evaluation of one's own abilities, actions, and values

self-esteem   a person's sense of his or her own worth

short-term goal   an objective that is achieved in a short period of time; usually supports long-term and intermediate goals

social networking sites   websites that allow people to link with friends, family, and colleagues through online networks

soft obligation   a task or commitment without a specific time frame or deadline

stress   a chemical response of the body to a perceived threat or danger

task list   a list of all the tasks an individual needs to accomplish in the day

team   a group of individuals working together to accomplish a common objective

teamwork   the act of working within a team setting, with individual members working toward a shared objective

temporary agency   an agency that places people in short-term job positions

time management plan   a system for planning time that includes assessing available time, setting priorities, and scheduling tasks

trade journal   a professional magazine devoted to one business or industry; presents industry-specific news and events as well as classifieds

traditional interview   a type of job interview in which the questions are mainly focused on an applicant's experience and skills; for example, "What are your biggest strengths and weaknesses?"

transcript   a record of academic achievement, usually including course titles and grades

transferable skills   skills learned in one situation that can be applied in another

unethical behavior   conduct that does not conform to accepted social or professional standards

values   a set of guiding principles for a group (such as a company) or an individual

verbal communication   communication that takes place through language, such as speech, writing, email, or texting

verbal offer   an offer of a job that is usually given over the phone or in person without a formal written agreement

warm leads   job leads that are publicly posted, just like cold leads, but for which the candidate knows someone who works at the organization

written offer   an official job offer that usually outlines the basic conditions of employment, including salary and benefits

Index